FOOD OF JAPAN
Published by
PERIPLUS EDITIONS (HK) LTD.,
with editorial offices at
153 Milk Street, Boston MA 02109
and 5 Little Road #08-01
Singapore 536983.

Copyright © 1998
Periplus Editions (HK) Ltd.

Hardcover ISBN: 962-593-392-1

Publisher: Eric Oey
Production: Mary Chia, Violet Wong
PRINTED IN SINGAPORE

Distributed by
USA/UK/Europe
Charles E. Tuttle Co., Inc.
RR 1 Box 231-5, North Clarendon,
VT 05759-9700
Toll Free Tel.: (800) 526-2778
Tel.: (802) 773-8930
Fax.: (802) 773-6993

Asia-Pacific
Berkeley Books Pte. Ltd.
5 Little Road #08-01
Singapore 536983
Tel.: (65) 280-3320
Fax.: (65) 280-6290

Acknowledgments
The publisher gratefully acknowl-
edges the generous assistance of the
following: Rakusai Takahashi and
Yasuhiro Kohara of Shigaraki Vil-
lage for the loan of hand-crafted
pottery; in Kobe, Akemi Scott, Seiko
Okamoto and D. Lavery for the
loan of beautiful antiques, ceramics
and fabrics; in Osaka, Kintetsu
Department Store for the loan of
various tableware; Akatorii, for pottery and fine ceramics; Hayashi, for
lacquerware; Antique Kirara, for antiques and *objets d'art*, and Gerti
Wagner for pottery and paintings.
Special thanks are due to Masako
Mitsuyoshi for translating the
recipes and to Executive Sous Chefs
Yuji Yazama and Armin Zahner for
their assistance in recipe testing, as
well as to Rosy Phua and Takashi
Baba for help in making props.
Lastly, thanks to Mrs. Ong for her
untiring work organizing and safe-
guarding the hundreds of valuable
prop items appearing in this book.

Photo Credits
Photos by Heinz von Holzen except
except pages 2, 15 by Eric Oey,
pages 6, 7, 10, 19 by Photobank,
page 8 by Dallas & John Heaton,
pages 9, 14, 20 by Ben Simmons.
Illustrations on pages 12 and 13
courtesy of Okura Shukokan
Museum, Tokyo and Tsuneo
Tamba Collection, respectively.

THE FOOD OF
JAPAN

Authentic Recipes from the Land of the Rising Sun

Recipes by *Takayuki Kosaki* & *Walter Wagner*

Food photography by *Heinz von Holzen*

Styling & Cover by *Christina Ong*

Introduction by *Kathleen Morikawa*

Edited by *Wendy Hutton*

Produced in association with the Hyatt Regency Osaka

PERIPLUS
EDITIONS

Distributed in the Continental United States by The Crossing Press

Contents

Part One: Food in Japan

Japanese food is "designed to be eaten with the eyes"

More than any other cuisine in the world, Japanese food is a complete aesthetic experience, a delight for the eyes, the nose and the palate. The desire to enhance rather than to alter the essential quality of fresh seasonal ingredients results in a cuisine that is unique, a tribute to nature and to man who, after all, produced the exquisite tableware on which the food is presented.

Japanese restaurants abroad were once frequented largely by homesick Japanese tourists or businessmen longing for a taste of home. Over the past couple of decades, however, Japanese cuisine has earned an international following and inspired the presentation of French *nouvelle cuisine* as well as a wave of Japanese-influenced dishes everywhere from Paris to San Francisco to Sydney. As palates become more adventurous and as health-conscious diners seek food that is low-fat, low in sugar and makes wide use of soy beans and vegetables, Japanese food is increasingly popular and ingredients are easier to obtain internationally.

Surrounded by seas rich in fish, the Japanese have made the bounty of the sea a vital part of their diet, eating a variety of seaweed as well as many different fish and shellfish. The basic stock of Japanese cuisine, *dashi*, is redolent of the sea, being made from dried kelp and dried bonito flakes.

There is a Japanese saying that a meal should always include "something from the mountain and something from the sea," the mountain being represented by a range of seasonal vegetables together with the staple, rice. Poultry and meat are also eaten, although are less important than the humble soy bean, which appears as nutritionally rich bean curd (*tofu*); as *miso*, fermented soy bean paste used for soups and seasoning, and, of course, in the form of the ubiquitous soy sauce.

A number of factors come together to form the main elements of Japanese cuisine. Seasonal and regional specialities set the overall tone for the meal. Historical influences can be seen in the choice of foods, preparation techniques and the custom of eating certain foods at certain times of the year. The presentation of food is always of paramount importance, with great care given to detail, color, form and balance. The food provides a showcase for the Japanese arts of porcelain, ceramics, basketware, lacquer and bamboo.

The secret to preparing Japanese cuisine at home is an understanding of the basic ingredients and of how a meal is composed, the culinary methods used are actually very simple. But the most important requirement of all is simply a love of good food prepared and presented with a sense of harmony.

Page 2
Early breakfast at a traditional inn on the slopes of Mount Fuji.
Opposite:
An array of tiny portions of exquisitely presented food typical of Japan's haute cuisine, kaiseki ryori.

The Paradox of Modern Japan

A country of physical contrasts where old and new coexist

Japan is a land of dramatic contrast: the traditional *geisha* using high-tech gadgetry; the much vaunted politeness and the elbow in the back on a crowded commuter train; the constant desire to "save face" balanced against the nation's love of the *karaoke* machine. *Kimono*, thatch-roofed farmhouses and views of Mount Fuji unobscured by skyscrapers are getting harder and harder to find, and yet if one scratches the shiny veneer of the new Japan, traditional ways and almost feudalistic values lie surprisingly close to the surface.

The old and the new, the traditional and the modern constantly clash and blend, adapting to and obliterating each other. Change is constant. Perhaps it is even a necessity in a nation which squeezes 124 million people (approximately half the population of the United States) into a land only slightly larger than Germany. Over 43 percent of the nation's population is crammed into the three major coastal metropolises of Tokyo, Osaka and Nagoya. Fully two-thirds of the land is mountainous or forested; only just over 14 percent is agricultural, a little over 4 percent for housing.

Adapting to ever-changing conditions, learning to work together in cooperative activities (such as rice cultivation and fishing), maintaining psychological rather than physical distance from others and following carefully prescribed rules of behavior have been traditionally accepted ways of dealing with life in a land where overcrowding and devastating earthquakes, typhoons, volcanic eruptions and landslides are common. In such an environment, permanence is a difficult quality to maintain and is, indeed, seldom sought. It is the fleeting moment and the fast-fading beauty of the cherry blossom that are esteemed.

Japan is also a land that, despite claims of homogeneity, is considerably diverse, with customs, festivals and dialects varying greatly from region to region. The country is composed of four main islands (Hokkaido, Honshu, Shikoku and Kyushu) and several thousand smaller islands stretching 1,900 miles from Hokkaido, whose northern shores

Traditional thatch-roof wooden farm houses, such as this one in Gifu Prefecture, are increasingly difficult to find.

minority who now live mainly on the northern island of Hokkaido. They were once hunters and fishermen who are thought to have roamed large areas of northern Honshu. With its rugged coastline and mountains and long snowbound winters, Tohoku in northern Honshu was traditionally considered one of Japan's most remote and least developed areas.

Central Japan encompasses the Sea of Japan coastal areas, where quiet fishing villages can still be found, and the Japan Alps region centered in Nagano Prefecture, sometimes nicknamed the Roof of Japan. Three major mountain ranges traverse Nagano, the site of the 1998 Winter Olympics and a mecca for tourists from eastern and western Japan. From the scenic Koumi train line running through central Nagano, it is possible to enjoy views of the Japan Alps, the still-active volcano Mount Asama and Mount Fuji in the distance.

face the Sea of Okhotsk, to Iriomote Island in the south near Taiwan and the Tropic of Cancer.

Hokkaido is the island which least conforms to the outsider's image of Japan. It is a land of wide expanses, dairy farms and ranches raising thoroughbred horses, and meadows of wildflowers and lavender, more reminiscent of the American Midwest than of the island of Honshu. The Ainu, the indigenous people of Japan, are a small Caucasoid

The 12,388-foot Mount Fuji is Japan's highest mountain and the sacred symbol of the nation. In summer, its peak attracts long lines of climbers determined to make the pilgrimage to the top at least once in their lives. Those hardy enough to succeed can hike around the crater, revive themselves with a bowl of curry rice at the restaurant on top and use the conveniently installed pay phone to talk to the folks back home before beginning their descent.

Railway lines crisscross the nation and the fastest and most famous is the Tokaido Shinkansen bullet train linking the major metropolises of the Pacific coast from Tokyo to Hakata on the island of Kyushu. Visitors to Japan's major cities are often dismayed by the grey, endless urban sprawl. The joy of traveling through urban Japan comes from the discoveries hidden along the way: an ancient castle painstakingly preserved and hiding behind a wall of high-rise office buildings, *tori* gates peeking out from behind a shopping center parking lot, or a tiny delicately manicured Japanese garden tucked around an otherwise nondescript corner.

At Kurashiki, along the Tokaido Shinkansen route in western Japan, tourists can escape from the congested roads and fast-food shops of modern Japan into the "old town" of the city. It is a peaceful quarter of canals linked by arched stone bridges and lined with willow trees, old granaries and shops of white plaster and black tile that evoke memories of earlier days. At its center stands the Ohara Museum of Western Art, its Greek temple facade an amusing contrast in the midst of this trib-

ute to Tokugawa Japan. After almost 150 years of contact with the outside world, Japan is a conglomerate of all it has absorbed and the distinctive old culture becomes more and more difficult to find in its original form.

Across the Inland Sea from Kurashiki on Shikoku, Japan's fourth largest island, a little of the old exoticism can be found in modern-day pilgrims dressed in the traditional costume of wandering monks—simple robes, prayers beads, straw hats, sandals and staffs—who circle the island's 88 holy temples on foot (or, for the less hardy, by bus or train) in search of enlightenment or as a way to come to terms with their problems or their past.

The southernmost province of Okinawa, comprised of 160 small islands, is checkered with fields of sugar cane and pineapples, war memorials and military bases, and boasts some of the nation's most beautiful beaches and coral reefs, yet is constantly battling to survive the threats of concrete piers and mainland tourist developers. Okinawa is culturally quite different from mainland Japan and was known as the independent kingdom of the Ryukyu Islands until the Satsuma Clan of Kyushu invaded in 1609. Even today, much of the islands' traditional culture, cuisine and music have been preserved.

Surrounded by seas rich in marine life, the Japanese prefer fish to meat or poultry. These ones that didn't get away are seen in Tokyo's Tsukiji fish market.

The serenity of some parts of Japan, as exemplified by this view of Mount Fuji, with Lake Ashi in the foreground, is in striking contrast to its intensely crowded and hectic cities.

gaged in trade and provided information on Western medicine, languages and science. This national policy of seclusion from the outside world led to the development of an exclusive, inward-looking mentality that occasionally raises its head even today.

The arrival of the American Commodore, Matthew Perry, in 1858, eventually forced open the doors of the long-closed society and in the century that followed, Japan engaged in a mad rush to catch up with the West. The first phase of this race modernised Japanese society but led to expansionism and defeat in World War II. The second phase gave birth to the unparalleled economic success of the post-war period.

Japan's success is largely attributable to its people: their

To the north of Okinawa, Kyushu, the third largest of Japan's islands, is renowned for its Imari and Arita pottery, its hot springs resorts and very active volcanoes. Nagasaki in western Kyushu was traditionally the center of trade with China and Holland and Japan's door to the outside world. During the Edo Period (1603–1867), only the Dutch were allowed to maintain a small settlement on the island of Dejima in Nagasaki Bay, from where they en-

perseverance and passive acceptance of fate, their vitality and determination to forge ahead and their ability to follow obediently. They have displayed the flexibility to turn the nation into the world's second largest superpower, yet cling to often inflexible rules and social behavior. The nation maintains ancient arts, crafts and traditions in the face of an increasingly high-tech world and yet is able to cope with constant change. Japan is truly a paradox.

The Evolution of Japanese Cuisine

Despite sharing many ingredients with its neighbors,
Japan has created and retained its unique cuisine

Japanese cuisine today is the result of two millennia of culinary influences imported from the outside world, refined and adapted to reflect local preferences in taste and presentation, resulting in a style that is uniquely Japanese.

Rice cultivation, believed to have come from China, began in Japan around 300 B.C. Rice was used as a form of tribute and taxation right up until the early 20th century and became a rare luxury for the farmers who produced it. They generally had to exist on barley, buckwheat and other grains.

Meat eating and milk drinking were common practices until the late 7th century, but as Buddhism emerged as an important force in the nation, restrictions were placed on the eating of meat. In the 8th century, meat-eating was officially prohibited and the forerunner of today's *sushi* appeared.

Chinese influence on the Japanese cuisine continued to be strong for the next three centuries. It was from China that Japan learned the art of making bean curd (*tofu*) and how to use chopsticks. China was also the origin of soy sauce, said to have come from the Asian mainland in the 8th or 9th century, although today's Japanese-style soy sauce is a product of the 15th century. Tea was first introduced from China in the 9th century, but gradually faded from use only to be reintroduced by a Zen priest in the late 12th century.

In the Heian Period (794–1185), Japan's distinctive style of cuisine began to develop. The capital was moved from Nara to Kyoto and the thriving aristocracy had the time to indulge its interests in art, literature, poetry, fine cuisine and elaborate games and pastimes. Elegant dining became an important part of the lifestyle and the aristocracy were not only gourmets but gourmands who supplemented their regular two meals a day with numerous between-meal snacks. Today, *Kyo ryori*, the cuisine of Kyoto, represents the ultimate in Japanese dining. This is exemplified by *kaiseki*, which features an assortment of carefully prepared and exquisitely presented delicacies.

In 1885, the government moved to Kamakura where the more austere *samurai* lifestyle and Zen Buddhism fostered a healthier, simpler cuisine. *Shojin ryori* (vegetarian Buddhist temple fare), heavily influenced by Chinese Buddhist temple cooking, features small portions of a wide variety of vegetarian foods prepared in one of five standard cooking methods. *Shojin ryori* guidelines include placing emphasis on food of five colors (green, red, yellow, white and black-purple) and six tastes (bitter, sour, sweet, hot, salty and delicate). It was an extremely important culinary influence during its time and this

emphasis on certain tastes, colors and cooking techniques lives on today. *Shojin ryori* also led to the development of *cha kaiseki*, food served before the tea ceremony, in the mid-16th century.

Japan's trade with the outside world from the 14th to 16th centuries brought many new influences. *Kabocha*, the much-loved green-skinned pumpkin, was introduced via Cambodia by the Portuguese in the 16th century. They were followed a century later by the Dutch, who introduced corn, potatoes and sweet potatoes. European cooking techniques created some interest and developed into what came to be known in Japan as "the cooking of the southern Barbarians" or *Nanban ryori*.

It is from the Portuguese *pao* that Japan derived its word for bread, *pan*. The Portuguese are credited with introducing *tempura* (batter-fried foods) as well as the popular cake *kasutera* (*castilla*). The culinary cross-cultural communication was not entirely one-sided; the Dutch are said to have taken soy sauce back to Europe with them.

During the Edo Period (1603-1857), Japan underwent almost three centuries of self-imposed seclusion from the outside world. The nation looked inward and a highly refined and very prosperous merchant class with the cash to pursue its sophisticated tastes in foods and the arts gradually arose. Noodle restaurants proliferated during this period and *nigiri-zushi* (seasoned rice wrapped in toasted seaweed) was invented.

The Meiji Period (1868–1912) marked the return of contact with the outside world. In the late 19th century, beef was once again allowed on the menu and the early 20th century brought growing interest in such foreign treats as bread, curry, ice cream, coffee and croquettes.

In the postwar period, purists have decried the decline of Japanese home cooking citing the electric rice cooker, instant noodles in styrofoam cups, instant *miso* soup, powdered *dashi* stock and ready-made pickling preparations that provide "homemade" pickles in minutes. Yet the numerous cooking programs on Japanese television and the number of cookbooks in the bookstores confirm that modern Japanese are still very much interested in the preparation of good food.

The Japanese desire to adapt outside influences to local tastes has never waned and has produced such unique blendings of East and West as green-tea ice cream, seaweed-flavored potato chips and cod-roe spaghetti. And deep is the shock of the visitor to Japan who bites into a frozen chocolate-colored ice, only to discover he has purchased an *azuki*, or red-bean, bar instead.

Left:
Foreigners enjoying Japanese food and, it would seem, sake.
Opposite:
A kitchen scene where cooks are preparing carp; note the unusual ladle made from a scallop shell in the right foreground.

Regional Favorites

Food preferences and produce vary from north to south

The drastic extremes in Japan's climate—from the very cold northern island of Hokkaido to the subtropical islands of Okinawa—result in regional cuisines that are as diverse as the land itself.

In Hokkaido, with its wide open spaces and climate that is not conducive to rice cultivation, the people have acquired a taste for potatoes, corn, dairy products, barbecued meats and salmon. Their own special version of Chinese noodles, called Sapporo *ramen*, is often served with a dab of butter. Seafood *o-nabe* (one-pot stews) featuring crab, scallops and salmon are also a speciality of the region.

There is a great difference in the food preferences of the residents of the Kanto region (centered around Tokyo and Yokohama) and the Kansai region (Kyoto, Osaka and environs). In the Kansai area, fermented soy bean soup, or *miso*, is almost white compared with the darker brown and red *miso* favored in the Kanto region. Eastern and Western Japan are also divided by differing tastes in *sushi*, sweets and pickles. The Kyoto area is identified with

the light, delicately flavored cuisine of the ancient court—true haute cuisine—and there is a feeling in Western Japan that in Tokyo, they are definitely a little heavy-handed with the soy sauce.

Nagoya, located halfway between Tokyo and Kyoto, is known for its flat *udon* noodles and *uiro*, a sweet rice jelly. Pilgrims visiting the Buddhist temples on Shikoku would be sure to try the island's famous Sanuki *udon* noodles, fresh sardines and mandarin oranges. Kyushu is known for its tea, fruits and seafood products, and for the Chinese and Western culinary influences that developed because of Nagasaki's role as a center of trade with the outside world. Visitors to that city make sure to taste an authentically rich *kasutera* (*castilla*) sponge cake.

On the islands of Okinawa, dishes featuring pork are favored. Sweets made with raw sugar, pineapples and papaya are also popular, as are several powerful local drinks: *awamori*, made from sweet potatoes, and *habu sake*, complete with a deadly *habu* snake coiled inside the bottle.

Each region has its own specialties, even when it comes to sushi, *seen here in an Osaka* sushi bar.

O-bento: A Portable Feast

*From the Rising Sun Flag Lunch to the Loving Wife's Lunch,
the o-bento is a microcosm of Japanese cuisine*

The *o-bento* or box lunch is a Japanese institution which consists of white rice and an assortment of tiny helpings of meat, fish, vegetables, egg, fruit and a pickled plum (*umeboshi*), all arranged in a small rectangular box.

The pickled plum is believed to aid digestion and is a method of keeping the rice from spoiling. If other ingredients are not available, an *o-bento* may consist only of a red pickled plum planted firmly in the center of a field of white rice, called a *hinomaru bento* or "Rising Sun flag lunch."

Since only small portions of each food are included and a well-balanced variety of foods is necessary, preparing a proper *o-bento* can be a time-consuming ritual. As with almost all Japanese dishes, attention to detail and attractive presentation are paramount.

A homemade *o-bento* is considered a tangible symbol of a wife's or mother's love and devotion. A young husband may be embarrassed by the time and tender loving care devoted to the preparation of the lunch box known as the *aisai bento* (loving wife's lunch) and be hesitant to eat it in front of colleagues. Children, less easily intimidated, glory and gloat over their lunch boxes. They compare and trade delicacies, demonstrating a sense of security and pride in the love of a mother who will bother to wake at 5 A.M. to fry chicken tidbits, make rectangular omelets, create panda bear and beagle faces out of seaweed and vegetables.

The most famous of the commercially made *o-bento* are the *ekiben*, the box lunches available at most of the nation's train stations. These vary greatly from one area of the country to another and are considered to be an important way of promoting regional delicacies, customs and crafts. In Takasaki, Gunma Prefecture, a region known for its doll-making industry, the lunch boxes are sold in little red plastic bowls shaped like a Daruma doll, the plastic cover resembling the face of the Daruma. It's a distinctive local touch that has made Takasaki's *ekiben* famous nationwide. For some travelers, tasting all the local *ekiben* along their route is a vital part of the trip.

Everyone enjoys a box lunch, from schoolchildren and businessmen to Buddhist monks.

The Fleeting Moment

Seasonal foods reflect Japan's cultural attitudes as well as shape its cuisine

One of the most striking aspects of Japanese cuisine is the emphasis on seasonal cuisine. Every food has its appropriate season, which not only ensures that Japanese tastes are in harmony with nature but that they enjoy the freshest possible seasonal ingredients.

Connoisseurs delight in the first appearance of any seasonal speciality and are eager to partake of the first bonito fish or new green tea in spring, or the first *matsutake* mushrooms or mackerel in autumn.

The Japanese year is filled with holidays and festivities that require special seasonal delicacies: appropriate sweets and sweet *sake* for the Doll Festival parties held for little girls on March 3rd and rice dumplings for moon-viewing parties in September.

By far the most important of seasonal dining specialities is *osechi ryori*, the special foods that are served during the first week of the new year. Dozens of items are decoratively arranged in tiered lacquer boxes which are brought out again and again over the first few days of the new year, providing housewives a little respite from the non-stop eating (and serving) that marks the holiday.

Customs vary from home to home and region to region, but the typical New Year foods usually include *kamaboko* fish sausages bearing auspicious bamboo, plum and pine designs, *konbu* seaweed rolls tied into bows with dried gourd strips, boiled black beans, chestnuts in a sticky sweet-potato paste, herring roe, shredded carrot and white radish in sweet vinegared dressing and pickled lotus root. Vegetables such as *shiitake* mushrooms, radishes, lotus root, carrots and burdock are boiled in a soy sauce and *dashi* broth. The savory steamed egg custard known as *chawan-mushi* is also often eaten at this time.

The staple accompaniment for these dishes is *o-mochi*, rice cakes that can be grilled or boiled in a soup called *o-zoni* served on New Year's morning. These chewy treats must be eaten carefully, for each year several elderly diners choke to death on their New Year *o-mochi*.

Right:
An array of mushrooms, which are eagerly sought during the autumn months.
Opposite:
Each season has its special foods. Restaurants and private homes change their serving dishes to suit the season, as in this autumnal spread.

Once, all families made their own rice cakes, but now it is a tradition that is chiefly maintained in the countryside. *Mochi-gome*, a special type of glutinous rice, is prepared and while it is still hot, molded into a ball and placed in a large round wooden mortar where it is pounded rhythmically. The final product is rolled out flat and cut into rectangular cakes. Nowadays, rural housewives freeze some of the cakes, which can be defrosted at short notice throughout the year when some special occasion arises.

Cherry blossoms signal the coming of spring, and in top restaurants diners may be served a cup of cherry blossom tea with several delicate blossoms floating in the clear, slightly salty beverage. Cherry blossom viewing parties are a seasonal must for the majority of Japanese. Lunch boxes, or *o-bento,* are packed full of delicacies to be eaten beneath the fragrant blossom, although at this time, the emphasis is most often on *o-sake* (the drink) rather than *o-bento* (the food).

Bamboo sprouts are another spring delicacy, as are the year's first bonito and rape blossoms. Spring is also the time when nature lovers take to the forests to hunt for edible wild plants such as bracken (*warabi*) and fiddleheads (*zenmai*).

Hot summer weather marks the time for eating grilled eel, which is believed to supply the energy needed to survive the sticky, humid weather. It is also the time for octopus, abalone and plenty of fresh fruits and vegetables, especially the summer favorite, *edamame*—fresh soy beans boiled in the pod, dusted with salt and popped into the mouth as the perfect accompaniment for beer on a hot summer's night. Another summer dining treat is cold noodles served with a *dashi* and soy sauce dip.

Strings of persimmon set out to dry can be seen dangling from the eaves of many a farmhouse in the countryside in autumn. This is also the season for roasted chestnuts, *soba* noodles made from freshly harvested and ground buckwheat, and for mushroom hunting. *Matsutake*, highly prized mushrooms savored for their distinctive fragrance, appear in autumn and connoisseurs crave seasonal soups and rice dishes flavored with this delicacy. *Matsutake* are most prevalent in the cold mountainous areas of central Japan and are so greatly valued that the mushroom marketing is big business in remote mountainous areas, where villagers struggle to defend their crops of "brown gold" from poachers. Their concern is easily understood when one realizes that *matsutake* can be sold for approximately $100 per pound in a normal year.

Late autumn is the time for preserving the year's vegetable harvest for winter. A large variety of pickling methods are popular in Japan, the most common using *miso* (fermented soy bean paste), salt, vinegar or rice bran as preservatives.

The onset of winter brings *fugu sashimi*, strips of raw blowfish which can be a deadly delicacy if the poison in the liver and ovaries is not removed correctly by a licensed chef. Other winter favorites include mandarin oranges and *o-nabe*, one-pot stews designed to warm the body on a cold winter's night. On the final day of the year, it is customary to eat special *soba*, for it is believed that the long noodles will guarantee health and longevity in the new year.

Bitter Sweet

The bitterness of Japanese tea is balanced by artistic sweets and dumplings

Few things are as quintessentially Japanese as the ritual tea ceremony which, for the non-Japanese, seems to encapsulate all the refinement, discipline and mystique of Japanese culture. *Cha-noyu*, the Way of Tea, began in the 15th century and in its early form, placed much emphasis on displaying and admiring imported Chinese art objects.

The Way of Tea gave rise to two of the more interesting aspects of Japanese cuisine: *cha kaiseki*, Japanese *haute cuisine* designed to be served as a light meal before a tea ceremony, and *wagashi*, traditional Japanese sweets which became an important accessory to the tea ceremony from the mid-16th century on. *Wagashi* today vary from the rather light treats enjoyed with a cup of pale green tea in the afternoon to the exquisitely delicate and often extremely sugary *wagashi* offered to neutralize the bitter taste of the powdered green tea.

Kanten, an agar agar-based gelatin, is an important ingredient in the sweets. When made into a jelly, *kanten* is a pliable sculpting material in the

hands of a skilled craftsman who can swiftly carve a pale purple portion of *kanten* into a beautiful hydrangea in full bloom in spring, or create goldfish afloat in a cool sea of jellied *kanten* in summer.

Due to their association with the tea ceremony and the ancient aristocracy, *wagashi* sometimes bear names that allude to the literature and poetry of the distant past.

Although there are some standard favorites available all year-round, most *wagashi* makers vary their products according to the changing seasons. *Sakura mochi*, a soft rice dumpling tinted cherry blossom pink, filled with bean jam and wrapped in a cherry tree leaf, is popular in spring time. *Kashiwa mochi*, a similar cake wrapped in an oak leaf, is eaten in May. Autumn foliage is replicated in October and snow-capped mountain designs take over in winter. In January, the Oriental zodiac's animal for that year makes an appearance.

A visit to a traditional Japanese sweet shop is indeed a treat for the eyes as well as the stomach.

The formal tea ceremony, with its bitter powdered green tea, led to the creation of delicate wagashi *sweets during the 10th century.*

Part Two: The Japanese Kitchen

Despite today's electric rice cooker, traditional bamboo utensils are still preferred

For hundreds of years, the Japanese kitchen was a simple dark room with a wood burner, a large crock for holding water, another crock or wooden tub for holding pickles and a wooden counter for cutting. These early kitchens were certainly not bright and pleasant places, but the process of cooking and eating together was made more cheerful by the use of the *irori*, a large open hearth heated with charcoal and positioned in the middle of the main room of the house. A hook hung above the hearth to hold a kettle of boiling water for tea, or for one of the one-pot stews that are an important part of Japanese home cooking. Fish and rice cakes were often grilled here too.

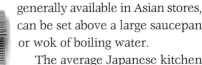

The Japanese kitchen took a major step forward in the early postwar period, and today the kitchen has modern electric appliances, including the all-important rice cooker. However, the basic utensils have changed very little and most cooks still prefer to use traditional utensils made from bamboo. These include a variety of bamboo baskets for draining noodles (a colander or sieve make an adequate substitute), a bamboo rolling mat and a bamboo steamer. The bamboo mats, which should be available in any specialty Asian kitchen store, are useful for rolling rice inside wrappers of seaweed (*nori-maki*), for rolling up Japanese omelets, for squeezing the liquid out of cooked vegetables and for a number of other tasks. Tiered bamboo steamers, generally available in Asian stores, can be set above a large saucepan or wok of boiling water.

The average Japanese kitchen will include a mortar and pestle used especially for grinding the sesame seeds that are a vital ingredient in many sauces and dressings; an electric blender is a good substitute. Other important items include a grater for radish, ginger and horseradish; a pan for deep frying (a wok is ideal); earthenware casserole pots and a variety of sharp knives for cutting meat, vegetables and fish for *sashimi*.

The most symbolic kitchen utensil, the *shamoji*, (the wooden scoop used to serve the rice), has come to represent domestic authority. When an older woman hands over her *shamoji* to her daughter-in-law, it symbolically represents her desire to hand over management of household affairs to the younger woman and is also an unspoken admission that the younger woman has finally passed muster.

Opposite:
The traditional open hearth or irori is virtually a museum piece in Japan today.
Centre:
A bamboo rolling mat is indispensable in a Japanese kitchen.
Below:
The wooden or bamboo rice scoop is a symbol of domestic authority as well as a practical way of dishing out steamed rice.

Planning and Presenting a Meal

The composition and presentation of Japanese meals is very different from that of other cuisines

The two extremes of Japanese cuisine are a full *kaiseki ryori*, an exquisite array of a dozen or more tiny portions of food artfully arranged on superb tableware, and the basic meal consisting merely of boiled rice, *miso* soup and pickles. Japanese cuisine developed out of austerity, and a sense of restraint rather than lavish display is still inherent in Japanese food today. Don't be misled into thinking that because the individual portions of the food that make a meal are small, you'll finish a Japanese meal hungry. With the variety of tastes, textures and flavors, you're certain to feel satisfied at the end of a meal.

The basis of every main meal in Japan is boiled rice, *miso* soup and pickles. Accompanying dishes are varied according to availability, season, how much time you have for preparation of the meal and so on. The Japanese do not categorize their food by the basic ingredient (for example, vegetables, beef or fish), but by the method with which it is prepared. Food is thus classified as grilled, steamed, simmered, deep-fried or vinegared. As this concept is unfamiliar to Western cooks, recipes in this book have been grouped to follow the basic pattern of a Japanese meal.

A Japanese meal can be divided into three main areas: a beginning, a middle and an end. The beginning includes appetizers, clear soups and raw fish (*sashimi*). The middle of the meal is made up of a number of seafood, meat, poultry and vegetables dishes prepared by either grilling, steaming, simmering, deep frying or serving as a vinegared "salad." To ensure variety, each style of preparation would be used only once for the foods making up the middle of the meal. For example, if the fish was deep fried, the vegetables might be simmered in seasoned stock, the meat grilled and a mixture of egg and savory tidbits steamed. Alternatively, this variety of "middle" dishes might be replaced by a hot-pot (*nabe*), a one-dish combination of vegetables, seafood, meat, bean curd and noodles. The meal concludes with rice, *miso* soup and pickles, together with green tea and fresh fruit.

If you are new to Japanese cuisine, you will probably want to keep the menu relatively simple. Thus, planning around the basic rice, soup and pickles, you might like to prepare one appetizer and a couple of other dishes using fish, meat, poultry or vegetables. You might even limit the meal to one simple appetizer and a one-pot dish such as *sukiyaki*, followed by the rice-soup-pickles. As you become more confident, you'll find it easier to prepare a greater number of dishes. Don't forget, however, that restraint is a very Japanese characteristic and that it is better to serve three carefully cooked, beautifully presented dishes than six less-than-perfect ones.

In private homes and many restaurants, all the dishes making up the meal are presented at the same time. At a formal meal, however, the appetizers arrive first, followed by the "middle" dishes, each served in the order dictated by their method of preparation, concluding with rice, soup, pickles, green tea and fruit.

The presentation of Japanese food is an art that encourages the cook's imagination and creativity. As a German visitor to Japan remarked around the turn of the century, "a person doesn't go to the table as in the West but the table is brought to them from the kitchen already set with food." Individual trays for each diner are set with an assortment of bowls and plates, together with a pair of chopsticks which are finely pointed at the ends (unlike Chinese chopsticks, which are rounded or even blunt).

The choice of tableware in Japan is influenced by the season as well as by the type of food being served. Restaurants stock four sets of tableware, one for each season, and even private homes have a wide assortment of tableware in different materials, shapes and sizes. Soup and plain rice are always served in round lacquer bowls with a lid, while basketware is preferred for deep-fried foods. Rustic pottery, fine porcelain, glass, and lacquered trays are all used as considered appropriate.

Generally speaking, foods which are round (such as pieces of rolled meat or slices of lotus root) are presented on rectangular or square plates, while square-shaped foods are likely to be served on round plates. Such imagination is shown in Japan, however, that plates and bowls are not just square, rectangular or round; they might be hexagonal, semi-circular, fan-shaped or resemble a leaf or a shell. No wonder a Japanese traveling in Europe last century dismissed Western food with the remark "every damn plate is round."

It is worth looking for Japanese tableware for your homecooked Japanese food, as it adds enormously to the total aesthetic experience. And just as the tableware is important, so too is the garnishing of the food. It has been said in Japan that "a person cannot go out naked in public, neither can food." That carefully placed spray of *kinome* leaves, that tiny sprig of *shiso* flowers, that bright red ball of grated *daikon* mixed with grated red chili are all an integral part of the dish being presented.

In most cases, garnishes are edible. If you are obliged to use a substitute that is similar in color and shape (alfalfa sprouts or very finely shredded cabbage for the maroon *benitade* sprouts, for example) you will not be able to duplicate the taste. This is not crucial, however, so feel free to select garnishes of tiny flowers and leaves that seem to enhance the particular dishes you are serving.

This typical Japanese meal shows the imaginative use of a range of lacquerware, ceramics, porcelain and basketware.

Japanese Ingredients

*Cooking Japanese food is easy once you
know the basic ingredients*

*Cotton & Silken
Bean Curd*

Benitade

Bonito

BAMBOO SHOOTS: Fresh bamboo shoots, available in spring time, have an infinitely superior flavor and texture to the canned variety, although the latter can be used as a substitute. Buy whole canned shoots rather than sliced shoots, and simmer in water for 5 minutes before using to remove any metallic taste. Store in the refrigerator covered in fresh water, changing it daily, for up to 10 days.

BEAN CURD: An important, low-fat, inexpensive source of protein, several types of curd made from soy beans are used in Japanese cuisine. The most common, and the one most readily available in Western countries, is called "cotton" or *momen tofu*. Use this type unless otherwise specified in the recipes in this book. **"Cotton" bean curd** is generally sold packed in water in containers of about 9 ounces in Japan. It is firmer and easier to handle than fine-textured **"silken" bean curd** (*kinu-goshi tofu*), which is usually added to soups or enjoyed chilled in summer. This type of bean curd is often available in plastic trays or rolls designed to be cut with a sharp knife while still in the plastic so it will keep its shape. **Deep-fried bean curd** or *aburage* is available in plastic bags and should be rinsed in boiling water to remove excess oil before using. A **grilled bean curd** (*yakidofu*), which has a speckled brown surface, is also sold in plastic bags.

BENITADE: Decorative maroon-colored sprouts used as a garnish, these have a slightly peppery taste. Substitute alfalfa sprouts, or, for a similar color, very finely shredded red cabbage.

BONITO, DRIED: Together with dried kelp, this is one of the essential components of Japanese stock, or *dashi*. Rock-hard dried bonito fish was traditionally shaved just before use, but today, shaved bonito flakes (*katsuo-bushi*) available in plastic bags are most commonly used, both for *dashi* and as a garnish (sometimes tossed lightly with a little soy sauce for additional flavor).

BURDOCK: A long, skinny root which should be put into water to stop it discoloring immediately after scraping off the skin. Enjoyed more for its texture than its rather bland flavor, burdock is often available in Japanese and health food stores abroad. Canned burdock could be used as a substitute.

CHRYSANTHEMUM LEAVES: Edible chrysanthemum leaves from a particular variety of this flowering plant are enjoyed for their distinctive flavor and bright green color. Often available in Asian markets abroad (they are also used in Chinese cuisine); spinach could be used as a substitute, although it lacks the taste of chrysanthemum leaves. Also called *shungiku*.

CLOUD EAR FUNGUS: Sometimes known as wood fungus, this crinkly greyish-brown dried fungus swells to many times its original size after soaking in warm water for a few minutes.

CUCUMBER: Japanese cucumbers are short, roughly 1 inch in diameter, and have a sweeter flavor and better texture than large cucumbers. This variety, known as Lebanese cucumbers in some countries, is often available in Asian markets or substitute English cucumbers.

DAIKON: Probably the most widely used vegetable in Japan, the venerable giant white radish can be as small as 8 inches or a huge fat 20-inch-long monster. It is shredded and used raw as a garnish; sliced and simmered or stir fried; finely grated and squeezed as a garnish, and mixed with finely grated red chili to make the garnish known as *akaoroshi* (which can also be made with cayenne powder or crushed red chili paste). It is also pickled and sold in jars. Used in Chinese and Korean cuisine as well as Japanese, the giant

white radish should be readily available in any Asian or health food market.

DASHI: This stock made from dried kelp and dried bonito flakes is the basis of countless Japanese soups and sauces. Instant *dashi* granules (*dashi-no-moto*) are sold in glass jars in Japanese stores and provide a practical alternative when small amounts of *dashi* are required. However, if you want the maximum flavor for a soup, it is recommended that you make your own *dashi* (recipe page 33) .

DEVIL'S TONGUE: A strange, greyish-brown mass made from a starchy root known as devil's tongue (*konnyaku*). It is sold in plastic bags, kept refrigerated. A type of noodles made from this starch, *shiritaki konnyaku*, is also available.

EGGPLANT: This vegetable is much smaller and thinner throughout Asia than its Western counterpart. Japanese eggplant are often no more than about 4 inches long. Use slender Asian or Japanese eggplant for all recipes in this book, as they are less bitter and have a better texture.

GINGER: Fresh ginger is widely used as a flavoring for Japanese food. The skin should always be scraped off before using. To make ginger juice, finely grate about 3 inches fresh ginger. Squeeze it little by little in a garlic press, or wrap in cheesecloth and squeeze to extract the juice. Depending on the age of the ginger (young ginger is far more juicy), you

Chrysanthemum

Young Ginger Shoots

Japanese Green Pepper

Kinome

Lotus Root

Mioga

Miso

Mitsuba

will obtain 1–2 tablespoons of juice. Pickled ginger (*beni-shoga* or *gari*), sometimes dyed red, is sold in jars and widely used as a garnish. Slender pink young ginger shoots are also pickled and sold in jars, and make a particularly decorative garnish.

GREEN PEPPER, JAPANESE: Tiny slender green peppers which have none of the spiciness of green chili peppers are used in Japan, 8 Japanese peppers being the equivalent to 1 large green bell pepper available in Western countries. The latter is closer in taste to Japanese peppers and makes a better substitute than deseeded green chilies.

HORSERADISH: Probably the most popular accompaniment of all, horseradish (*wasabi*) is widely available as a ready mixed paste in tubes, although *wasabi* powder (available in tiny cans) mixed with a little water 10 minutes before required gives a much closer approximation of the freshly grated root.

KELP: see Seaweed

KINOME: Tender sprigs of leaves from the prickly ash tree have a decorative appearance and distinctive taste that makes them a popular garnish during the warmer months. Often available in Japanese stores, they will keep refrigerated for about 1 week. Although the flavor is different, sprigs of watercress make an acceptable substitute.

LOTUS ROOT: The bulb of the lotus plant has a delicious crunchy texture and very decorative appearance when sliced, making it a popular vegetable and garnish in Japan. Available fresh in many Asian stores; the canned version lacks the texture of the fresh root but can be used as a substitute.

MIOGA BUD: This pretty pale pink bud with green tips, a member of the ginger family, has no substitute; it is used for its spicy flavor and appearance in some Japanese dishes.

MIRIN: A very sweet rice wine sold in bottles in Japanese stores, this is used only for cooking, the alcohol often burned off by heating. If *mirin* is not available, use 1 teaspoon sugar as a substitute for 1 tablespoon *mirin*.

MISO: A protein-rich salty paste of fermented soy beans with a distinctive aroma and flavor, this is a very important ingredient in Japanese cuisine. Plastic bags or tubs of *miso* are generally sold in the refrigerated section of Japanese or health food stores; *miso* keeps refrigerated for up to 1 year. Many different types of *miso* are available, varying in taste, texture, color and fragrance. The most common found outside Japan are: **red *miso***, which has a reddish-brown color and an emphatic flavor, and is used for winter soups and other dishes, and **white *miso***, which is actually a golden-yellow color, has a lighter flavor and is less salty than the red variety. White *miso* is good for both soups and dressings. Other varieties such as **moro miso** and **inaka miso** ("country" *miso*) may be available in specialty stores; if not, use red *miso* as a substitute.

MITSUBA: Both the stems and leaves of this decorative herb, a member of the parsley family, are used in Japanese cuisine; parsley makes an acceptable substitute, although the flavor of *mitsuba* is more like celery.

MUSHROOMS: The mushroom season is eagerly awaited in Japan, where fresh wild mushrooms are highly sought after. There are also many commercially grown mushrooms. **Fresh *shiitake*** have an excellent flavor and are increasingly available outside Asia. **Dried *shiitake***, the brownish-black dried mushrooms also used in Chinese cuisine, are widely available in Asian stores. **Golden** or ***enoki* mushrooms** (*enokitaki*), clusters of slender cream-colored stalks with tiny caps, are sometimes available fresh, as well as canned; the tough end of the stems must be discarded before use. **Oyster mushrooms** (*maiitake*) are also available fresh or canned. Reddish-brown ***nameko* mushrooms** have a slippery texture and attractive reddish-brown cap; as their season is short, they are more commonly found in jars or cans. Similar to the *nameko* in size and shape, ***shimeji* mushrooms** lack their slippery texture.

MUSTARD: Prepared Japanese mustard, which is quite hot and similar to English mustard, is available in tubes. Alternatively, canned Japanese mustard powder can be mixed with a little water just before use. Do not substitute French or American mustards, which are either too sweet or too vinegary.

NOODLES: Noodles made from different basic ingredients are enjoyed both hot or cold in Japan. The common **wheat flour noodle**, *udon*, comes in various widths and is either flat or round. Packets of dried *udon*, whitish-beige in color, are readily available in Japanese stores. ***Somen*** are also made of wheat, but are very fine and white in color. ***Soba* noodles** made from buckwheat flour have a distinctive taste and are sometimes flavored with green tea, in which case their normal beige-brown color is replaced by green. Dried *soba* noodles are available in packets. Fine white **rice vermicelli** noodles or *hiyagumi* are virtually identical with those used in Chinese cuisine. Slippery bleached white **devil's tongue noodles** (*shirataki konyyaku*) can be replaced with **cellophane noodles**, which are made of mung bean flour and which should be soaked in hot water until they swell and become transparent.

NORI: see Seaweed

PONZU: A small lime known abroad as musk lime or by its Filipino name, *kalamansi*, this has a pleasant fragrance and less acidity than lemon or lime juice. The latter could be used, mixed with a little orange juice if liked.

POTATO: *Yamato-imo*, often referred to as a potato in Japan, is actually a type of mountain

Shiitake Mushrooms

Nameko & Shimeji Mushrooms

Enokitaki Mushrooms

Sato-imo Potatoes

Seaweed—Kelp

Seaweed—Wakame

Shiso Leaf

Shiso Flower

yam which is grated and used raw for its gluey texture and bright white color. Suitable substitutes are suggested in individual recipes in this book. *Sato-imo* potato is also a type of yam which has a much finer texture and slightly different flavor from Western potatoes. New potatoes make an acceptable substitute.

RED-BEAN JAM: Small red azuki beans are simmered, puréed and sweetened to make a type of jam known as *an*, used in many cakes.

RICE: Short-grained rice with a somewhat sticky texture is used in Japan; it is much easier to eat with chopsticks than other varieties. Do not serve fragrant Thai or Basmati rice with Japanese food as the combination of such distinctively flavored varieties with Japanese dishes does not give an authentic result.

SAKE: Popular as a drink, *sake,* or rice wine, is available in many different qualities and is also an important ingredient in cooking. It is almost always heated to get rid of the alcohol for Japanese cuisine. Widely available in liquor stores or in supermarkets where licensing laws do not prevent its sale, a bottle of *sake* will keep for about a month after opening. If red *sake* is not available, substitute regular *sake*.

SANSHO: A peppery powder made from the seeds of the prickly ash, available in small glass bottles in Japanese stores. If you can't find it, grind the dried Sichuan (Szechuan) pepper used in Chinese cuisine, as it is exactly the same seed ground for *sansho*.

SEAWEED: Important for flavoring and the minerals they contain, a variety of seaweeds is used in Japan. The most important is **dried kelp** or *konbu*, an essential ingredient in basic stock or *dashi*. Sold in packets, this has a dark green color, often with whitish patches on it. Wipe it clean with a damp cloth but do not soak before using. A special fine **golden kelp** (*shiraita konbu*) is also used on occasion. Small squares of **salted dried kelp** (*shio-kobu*), available in plastic packets, are enjoyed as a snack or used as a savory accent in some dishes. A type of seaweed generally referred to as **laver** (*nori*) is dried and sold in very thin, dark green sheets often already toasted so that it is crisp; it is sometimes available already shredded. *Wakame*, sold either dried (when it looks like a mass of large crinkly black tea leaves) or in salted form in plastic bags, is reconstituted by soaking in water. It has a pleasant chewy texture and subtle flavor that goes well in soups and appetizers. Fine hair-like shreds of a variety known as *mozuku* are sold in plastic packets in the refrigerated section of Japanese stores. Drain off any water before mixing with dressing. Some brands are already marinated with *tosa* vinegar and ready to eat.

SESAME: Both black and white sesame seeds, the latter more common, are used in Japan. White sesame seeds are toasted and crushed to make a paste; if you don't want to do this yourself, you can buy either a Chinese or Japanese brand of sesame paste. Middle-

Eastern *tahina* has a slightly different flavor as the sesame seeds have not been toasted before grinding; smooth peanut butter is a better substitute.

SEVEN-SPICE POWDER: A mixture of several different spices and flavors, *shichimi* contains *sansho*, ground chilies, hemp seeds, dried orange peel, flakes of *nori* and white sesame seeds and white poppy seeds. A mixture of several types of chilies and spices, *shichimi togarashi*, is a hotter, spicier condiment. Both are available in small bottles in Japanese stores.

SHISO: The tangy, attractive green leaves of the *Perilla frutescens* or beefsteak plant, related to the mint family, are a common garnish in Japan. There is no substitute for the flavor of *shiso* leaf, although any other decorative leaf could be used as a garnish. The decorative small flower sprig of *shiso* is often used as a garnish. Any small edible flower sprig, such as flowering basil, can be used as a substitute. The tiny seeds of *shiso* are used in some recipes; if these are not available, omit as there is no good substitute.

SOUR PLUMS: Salty pickled plums (*umeboshi*), which manage to retain their fruity fragrance, are very popular with plain rice as part of breakfast in Japan, and are believed to aid digestion. These dull-red plums are available in jars, and should be refrigerated after opening.

SOY SAUCE: Look for a Japanese brand of soy sauce; Kikkoman is widely regarded as one of the best and is readily available internationally. Soy sauce comes in various grades. Most frequently used is **light soy sauce**, which is saltier and has a lighter color and thinner texture than **dark soy sauce**; Chinese brands of dark soy could be used for the latter. Another type of soy sauce, **tamari**, is very strong, thick and black and should be available in Japanese and health food stores; substitute dark soy sauce if *tamari* is not available.

SPRING ONION: Several types of green onion and leek are used; as Japanese onions are seldom available overseas, spring onions, or scallions, are recommended throughout this book.

VINEGAR, RICE: Rice vinegar, less acidic than the malt or wine vinegars found in the West, has a pleasant mild fragrance. It is widely available overseas, although slightly diluted cider vinegar can be substituted for it.

WAKAME: see Seaweed

WASABI: see Horseradish

YUZU ORANGE: A citrus fruit that is orange colored but used only for its fragrant rind, this is unlike any other citrus found outside Japan. Lemon or lime rind could be used as a substitute, or if you are able to obtain the fragrant kaffir lime (*magrut* or *limau purut*) used in Thai and some Malaysian dishes, this could be used as an alternative.

Shichimi & Togarashi

Spring Onion

Sour Plums

Yuzu Orange

Sweetfish

Tile Fish

Flounder

Crab

Pufferfish

Lobster

Redfish

Bonito

Bream

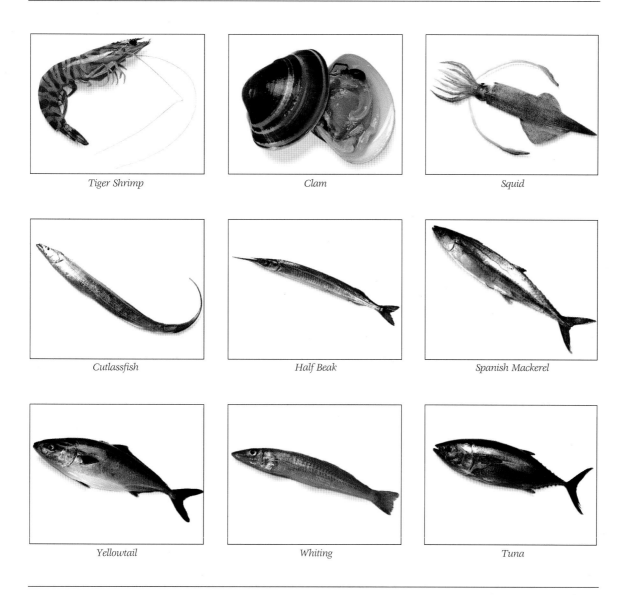

Tiger Shrimp

Clam

Squid

Cutlassfish

Half Beak

Spanish Mackerel

Yellowtail

Whiting

Tuna

Part Three: The Recipes

Basic recipes for stocks, sauces, vinegars and pickles precede those for main dishes, which begin on page 40

Katsuo Dashi • *Basic Dashi Stock*

$2^{1}/_{2}$-inch x $1^{1}/_{2}$-inch piece dried kelp (*konbu*)
$1^{1}/_{2}$ ounces dried bonito flakes (about 4 cups)
7 cups water

Wipe the kelp with a damp cloth, then put it in a saucepan with the water. Bring to a boil uncovered; just before the water comes to a boil, remove and discard the kelp. Sprinkle in the bonito flakes and remove the saucepan from the heat. As soon as the bonito flakes start to sink, strain the stock and discard the bonito flakes. This stock, which is the basis of many sauces and soups, can be kept refrigerated for up to 3 days.

Note: Instant *dashi* granules (*dashi-no-moto*) make a quick alternative if small amounts of the stock are needed; however, for soups and stock for simmered dishes, it is preferable to make your own *dashi*.

Happo Dashi • *Stock for Vegetables*

$^{2}/_{3}$ cup Basic *Dashi* Stock (see above)
4 teaspoons light soy sauce
$2^{1}/_{2}$ teaspoons *mirin*

Put the basic *dashi* stock in a saucepan and bring to a boil. Add the soy sauce and *mirin*, return to a boil, then remove from heat and allow to cool if not using immediately. This stock is often used for sim-

Ingredients

When recipe lists a hard-to-find or unusual ingredient, see pages 24 to 29 for possible substitutes. If a substitute is not listed, look for the ingredient in your local Chinese or local Asian food market, or check the mail-order listings on page 130 for possible sources.

Time Estimates

Time estimates for preparation only.

⏱ *quick and very easy to prepare*

⏱⏱ *relatively easy; less than 15 minutes' preparation*

⏱⏱⏱ *takes more than 15 minutes to prepare*

Main Dishes are intended to serve 4.

Opposite:
Clockwise from top: Shiba-zuke *Pickles; Pickled Eggplant; Salt-Pickled Turnip; Garlic in* Miso *and Pickled Cabbage & Carrot (center).*

mering green vegetables, and can be kept refrigerated for up to 3 days.

Soba Dashi (1) • *Stock for Hot Soba Noodles*

$^2/_3$ **cup Basic** *Dashi* **Stock (page 33)**
2 teaspoons light soy sauce
$^1/_2$ **teaspoon** *mirin*

Put all ingredients into a saucepan, bring to a boil and remove from the heat immediately. Serve with hot *soba* noodles. Keeps refrigerated for 2 days.

Soba Dashi (2) • *Stock for Cold Soba Noodles*

2 cups Basic *Dashi* **Stock (page 33)**
7 tablespoons dark soy sauce
7 tablespoons *mirin*

Put all ingredients into a pan, bring to a boil and remove from heat immediately. Skim the surface and allow to cool. Serve with cold *soba* noodles. Keeps refrigerated for up to 4 days.

Suiji • *Clear Soup*

$2^1/_2$ **cups Basic** *Dashi* **Stock (page 33)**
1 teaspoon light soy sauce
1 teaspoon salt
$^1/_2$ **teaspoon** *sake*

Put the stock, soy sauce and salt into a saucepan and heat until it comes almost to a boil. Remove from the heat immediately and add the *sake*. A variety of ingredients can be added to this clear soup, such as small cubes of silken bean curd, clams, shrimp, diced fish, sliced spring onions, *wakame* seaweed, mushrooms, cooked carrot slices, etc.

SAUCES

Tempura Dashi • *Tempura Dipping Sauce*

14 tablespoons Basic *Dashi* **Stock (page 33)**
$2^1/_2$ **tablespoons light soy sauce**
$2^1/_2$ **tablespoons** *mirin*

Put the basic *dashi* stock in a saucepan, bring to a boil and add soy sauce and *mirin*. Remove from heat immediately and serve hot as a dipping sauce for *tempura*.

Tosa Shoyu • *Tosa Soy Sauce*

$1^1/_2$ **tablespoons red** *sake*
$1^1/_2$ **tablespoons regular** *sake*
$1^3/_4$ **cups dark soy sauce**
$^1/_3$ **cup** *tamari* **soy sauce**
$^1/_2$ **ounce (about** $1^1/_3$ **cups) dried bonito flakes**
5-inch x 2-inch piece dried kelp (*konbu***)**

Put both types of *sake* in a small pan and bring to a boil to remove the alcohol. Allow to cool, then combine with all other ingredients and store for 1 week before straining. Can be stored for up to 1 year. Use as a dipping sauce for *sashimi*.
Note: If red *sake* is not available, use 3 tablespoons of regular *sake*.

Sakana Tare • *Fish Sauce*

$^2/_3$ **ounce bone from sea bream or other white fish**
$2^1/_2$ **tablespoons dark soy sauce**
$3^1/_2$ **tablespoons** *sake*
$2^1/_2$ **tablespoons** *mirin*
5 teaspoons sugar

Wash and dry the bone, then grill until any flesh clinging to it turns whitish. Put all other ingredients in a pan, add the fish bone and bring to a boil. Lower the heat, skim the surface and cook until the mixture has reduced by about 10 percent. Remove from heat. This sauce can be used to brush on fish when grilling.

Tori Tare • *Chicken Yakitori Sauce*

8 ounces chicken bones
2$^1/_2$ cups *sake*
$^2/_3$ cup dark soy sauce
1 cup *tamari* soy sauce
$^1/_2$ cup sugar

Wash chicken bones under running water, drain and grill until any flesh clinging to the bones turns whitish. Put the *sake* in a saucepan and bring to a boil to remove the alcohol. Add the bones and remaining ingredients and simmer until reduced by one-third. Skim the surface, strain and keep refrigerated for up to 1 month. This sauce is used to brush on chicken *yakitori*.

Kimi Shoyu • *Egg and Soy Sauce*

2 egg yolks
2 teaspoons light soy sauce

Beat the egg yolks well in a bowl. Add the soy sauce little by little and mix well. Make just before needed as an egg wash to obtain an attractive yellow color on grilled cuttlefish or squid.

Goma Tare • *Sesame Dipping Sauce*

Basic Sesame Paste:
18 ounces white sesame seeds (about 4 cups)
$^3/_4$ cup ground sesame paste or smooth peanut butter
1$^1/_2$ cups dark soy sauce
$^1/_2$ cup light soy sauce
$^1/_2$ cup cider vinegar
1 tablespoon sugar
3 tablespoons *mirin*

Sesame Sauce for Dipping:
1$^3/_4$ cups basic sesame paste (see above)
1$^1/_4$ cups Basic *Dashi* Stock (page 33)

To make the **basic sesame paste**, toast the white sesame seeds in a dry frying pan until golden brown. Put the toasted seeds, while still warm, into a blender and grind until you get a flaky paste. You will need to keep pushing the mixture back from the edges of the blender (Japanese chefs use a chopstick) during grinding. Put into a bowl and mix in all other ingredients, blending well. Keeps refrigerated for 3–4 months. To make the **sesame sauce for dipping**, combine the basic sesame paste with *dashi*. This will keep refrigerated for only 2–3 days.

Ponzu • *Citrus Sauce*

3-inch x 2$\frac{1}{2}$-inch piece dried kelp (*konbu*)
1$\frac{3}{4}$ cups musk lime (*ponzu* or *kalamansi*) juice,
or lemon juice
1$\frac{3}{4}$ cups dark soy sauce
$\frac{1}{3}$ cup *mirin*
$\frac{1}{4}$ cup *tamari* soy sauce
1$\frac{1}{2}$ ounces dried bonito flakes (about 4 cups)

Heat the dried kelp over a gas flame or under a broiler, then put into a bowl with all other ingredients. Refrigerate for 3 days, then strain. Can be stored for up to 1 year. (Bottled *ponzu* can be purchased in Japanese stores.)

VINEGARS

Tosa-zu • *Tosa Vinegar*

2 cups water
3-inch x 2$\frac{1}{2}$-inch piece dried kelp
(*konbu*)
1$\frac{1}{2}$ cups rice vinegar
2$\frac{1}{2}$ tablespoons light soy sauce
4 teaspoons dark soy sauce
4 teaspoons *mirin*
5 tablespoons sugar
1 teaspoon salt
1$\frac{1}{2}$ ounces dried bonito flakes (about 4 cups)

Put the water, kelp, vinegar, both types of soy sauce and *mirin* into a saucepan and heat. Just before it comes to a boil, remove the kelp and add sugar and salt. Stir to dissolve and bring to a boil. Remove from the heat and add bonito flakes. Cool, then strain. Keeps refrigerated for up to 1 week.

Kimizu • *Egg Yolk Vinegar*

5 egg yolks
$\frac{1}{3}$ cup *Tosa* Vinegar (see above)
Few drops of rice vinegar
Pinch of sugar
$\frac{1}{4}$ teaspoon salt

Beat the egg yolks in a bowl, then add remaining ingredients and mix. Put the mixture in a double boiler or heat-proof bowl and stand over simmering water. Beat with a whisk until the sugar and salt are dissolved. Chill over iced water.

Amazu • *Sweet Vinegar*

2 cups water
1 cup plus 2 tablespoons rice
vinegar
10 tablespoons sugar
2 teaspoons salt

Bring water and vinegar to a boil in a saucepan, then add sugar and salt and stir until dissolved. Remove from heat. Cool and use as a dipping sauce for vegetables. Keeps refrigerated up to 10 days.

Nanban-zu • *Nanban Vinegar*

2 cups Basic *Dashi* Stock (page 33)
$\frac{1}{2}$ cup rice vinegar
4 tablespoons light soy sauce
2$\frac{1}{2}$ teaspoons dark soy sauce
3 teaspoons *mirin*
5 tablespoons sugar

Put the *dashi* and vinegar into a saucepan and heat. Add both types of soy sauce and *mirin* and bring to a boil. Add sugar and stir until dissolved. Remove from the heat, cool and refrigerate for up to 10 days. Use as a marinade for fried fish.

MISCELLANEOUS

Dengaku Miso

1 pound red or white *miso* (1³/₄ cups)
¹/₃ cup *sake*
¹/₃ cup *mirin*
3 tablespoons sugar

Put all ingredients into a saucepan, preferably nonstick, and heat slowly, stirring from time to time. When it has come to the boil, reduce heat to a minimum and cook, stirring from time to time, for 20 minutes. Cool and refrigerate for up to 1 month.

Hoba Miso

2¹/₂ tablespoons *sake*
¹/₂ cup red *Dengaku Miso* (see above)
2 tablespoons *inaka miso*

Heat *sake* in a saucepan and simmer for a few seconds to remove the alcohol. Add both types of *miso*, mix and refrigerate for up to 1 month. Can be used to brush on scallops or fish before grilling.

Tamago-no-moto • *Japanese Mayonnaise*

3 egg yolks
¹/₂ teaspoon lemon juice
3 tablespoons white *miso*
1 cup salad oil
Salt to taste
Sprinkle of white pepper
A pinch of grated *yuzu*, lime or lemon peel

Beat the egg yolks and lemon juice with a wooden spoon in a bowl. Continue beating, adding the salad oil a few drops at a time until the mixture begins to emulsify. Keep on adding the oil until it is used up, then stir in the *miso* and season with salt, pepper and grated peel.

Tempura Ko • *Tempura Batter*

2 egg yolks
1 cup plus 2 tablespoons iced water
1³/₄ cups white flour, sifted

Put the egg yolks in a bowl and mix in the water gradually. Add the flour all at once and stir briefly (preferably with a pair of chopsticks), leaving in any lumps. Be sure not to mix the batter to a smooth paste; a *tempura* batter should contain lumps of dry flour. The mixture can be refrigerated until required, although it is best made immediately before it is needed.

Sushi-meshi • *Vinegared Rice*

4 cups short-grain rice
5 cups water
2¹/₄-inch square dried kelp (*konbu*)

Dressing:
¹/₂ cup rice vinegar
3 tablespoons sugar
5 teaspoons salt

Wash the rice gently under running water, taking care not to crush the grains, until the water runs clear. Leave the rice to drain in a colander for about 1 hour. Put in a saucepan with the water and kelp and bring to a boil over high heat. Reduce to medium heat and simmer for about 15 minutes, until the rice is cooked and the water has been absorbed. Turn off the heat. Remove the lid and cover the top of the pan with a towel to absorb any condensation. Put back the lid and leave the covered saucepan to one side for 20 minutes.

While the rice is cooking, mix the dressing ingredients in a small bowl, stirring until the sugar has dissolved, then set aside. Put the cooked rice in a wide wooden tub or plastic bowl. Stir gently in a circular motion with a rice paddle or wooden spoon, sprinkling in the dressing little by little, until it has been absorbed. Ideally, the rice mixture should be fanned to help cool it while the dressing is being stirred in.

Cover the bowl containing the vinegared rice with a damp cloth until it is needed for *sushi*. Keep at room temperature, not in the refrigerator, and use within 12 hours.

PICKLES

Nasu No Shiomomi • *Pickled Eggplant*

$3/_4$ **pound eggplant**
4 teaspoons salt
$1/_2$ **teaspoon toasted white sesame seeds**

Wash the eggplant but do not peel. Cut into $1/_2$-inch slices, sprinkle with salt and set aside for 10 minutes. Squeeze out the moisture and mix with toasted sesame seeds (if using). Serve with rice.

Kabu No Misozuke • *Turnips Pickled in Miso*

1 pound fresh turnips or *daikon*
4 teaspoons salt
1 cup *inaka miso*
3 tablespoons plus 1 teaspoon *sake*
2 tablespoons plus 2 teaspoons sugar

Peel the turnip or *daikon*, remove and set aside the green stalks and cut the vegetables into wedges. Sprinkle the vegetables with salt and keep for 2–3 hours.

Mix the *miso* with *sake* and sugar and add to the salted vegetables and the reserved green stalks. Marinate for 3 hours. Remove vegetables and stalks from the *miso*, cut in slices and arrange on a small plate.

Kyabetsu To Ninjin No Asazuke • *Pickled Cabbage and Carrot*

$3/_4$ **pound cabbage**
1 medium-sized carrot
$1/_4$ **English cucumber**
1 teaspoon toasted white sesame seeds
5 tablespoons salt

Cut cabbage in pieces about $1\frac{1}{4}$ inch square. Wash and drain. Peel carrot and cut into matchsticks about $1\frac{1}{4}$ inches long. Sprinkle the cucumber with salt, rubbing it into the skin with the fingers. Wash the cucumber, halve lengthwise and remove the seeds. Cut cucumber the same size as the carrot.

Put the prepared vegetables into a bowl, add the salt and cover with a small plate held down by a heavy weight. Leave overnight.

Chop the sesame seeds with a knife or crush lightly in a mortar. Sprinkle over the pickles just before serving with rice.

Shiba-zuke • *Shiba-zuke Pickles*

$^3/_4$ **pound eggplant**
1 English cucumber
5 ounces *shiso* **seeds (optional)**
$3^1/_2$ **ounces** *mioga* **bud**
6 teaspoons salt
2 teaspoons light soy sauce

Cut the eggplant in half lengthwise and then into pieces $1^1/_2$ inches long. Cut the cucumber into wedges, sprinkle with 1 teaspoon of the salt and rub gently. Rinse and dry.

Thinly slice the *mioga* diagonally, sprinkle with 1 teaspoon salt and squeeze gently to remove moisture. Pat dry. Pour hot water on the *shiso* seeds and soak until soft. Wash well, then drain.

Place the vegetables, seeds, *mioga* bud, remaining 4 teaspoons salt and soy sauce in a bowl, mix well and cover with a lid and a weight to press for half a day. Can be kept refrigerated for up to 3 days.

Ninniku Miso-zuke • *Garlic in Miso*

5 ounces garlic (about 3 whole bulbs)
1 teaspoon salt
$^3/_4$ **cup** *inaka miso*
4 tablespoons sugar

Peel the garlic and sprinkle with salt. Keep aside for 3 hours, then pat dry. Mix the *miso* with the sugar until dissolved, then add the garlic. Marinate for 4 days before serving with rice.

Gari • *Pickled Ginger*

8 ounces young ginger
6 tablespoons rice vinegar
2 tablespoons *mirin*
2 tablespoons *sake*
5 teaspoons sugar

Brush the ginger under running water, then blanch in boiling water for 1 minute. Drain.

Put the vinegar, *mirin*, *sake* and sugar in a small saucepan and bring to a boil, stirring until the sugar dissolves. Allow to cool.

Put the ginger into a sterilized jar and pour over the cooled vinegar. Cover and keep 3–4 days before using. This will keep refrigerated for up to 1 month.

Pickled ginger, which will develop a pale pink color as it ages, is sliced and served with *sushi* and a number of other Japanese dishes.

IKA KIMI YAKI & WAKATAKE SUI

Golden Cuttlefish & Clear Bamboo Shoot Soup

GOLDEN CUTTLEFISH

An egg wash gives the cuttlefish an attractive golden exterior. ☉ ☉

- ½ **pound cuttlefish tubes (squid may be substituted)**
- ¼ **teaspoon salt**
- **4 egg yolks, lightly beaten**
- **1 ounce tiny dried anchovies**
- **2 teaspoons** *mirin*
- **1 tablespoon sugar**
- **2 teaspoons dark soy sauce**
- **4 teaspoons water**
- **Seven-spice powder (*shichimi*) to taste**

Opposite:
Golden Cuttlefish
with a garnish of
fried anchovies
(below) and Clear
Bamboo Soup.

Make incisions in the cuttlefish ¼ inch apart. Skewer the cuttlefish and sprinkle with salt. Cook over a moderately hot charcoal fire or under a broiler for 7 minutes.

Brush the egg yolk on the cuttlefish and continue grilling for another 5 minutes, brushing with egg yolk another 3–4 times during the cooking. Cut into slices ½ inch thick.

If using very tiny anchovies no more than 1½ inches long, there is no need to remove the heads. If you have larger fish, remove the heads and extract any black interior. Put the anchovies into a nonstick pan and cook over low heat for 15 minutes, shaking the pan from time to time. Combine all other ingredients in a small pan, bring to a boil and simmer until the liquid is reduced by half. Add anchovies and stir until well coated with the liquid. Sprinkle with seven-spice powder and serve as a garnish for the cuttlefish.

CLEAR BAMBOO SHOOT SOUP ☉

- **4 medium-sized shrimp (about 3 ounces), peeled and halved lengthwise**
- **2 teaspoons cornstarch**
- **3 cups Clear Soup (page 34)**
- **1 ounce Simmered Bamboo Shoots (page 52), sliced (¼ cup)**
- **2½ ounces** *wakame* **seaweed**
- **Sprigs of** *kinome*, **watercress or parsley**

Shake the shrimp and cornstarch in a plastic bag, then put shrimp in a sieve and shake to dislodge excess cornstarch. Blanch shrimp in boiling water for about 20 seconds, until the cornstarch sets. Remove immediately, plunge in iced water for a few seconds, then set aside.

Pour the clear soup in a pan, add the bamboo shoots, bring to a boil, then add the shrimp and the *wakame*. Return to a boil and immediately remove from the heat. Divide the bamboo shoots, *wakame* and shrimp among 4 lacquer bowls and pour over the soup. Garnish with the *kinome*, watercress or parsley and serve at the beginning of a meal.

KAMO TSUMIRE & KARASHI RENKON
Soup with Duck Dumplings & Stuffed Lotus Root

SOUP WITH DUCK DUMPLINGS ◔◔

3 cups Basic *Dashi* Stock (page 33)
$^1/_2$ teaspoon salt
2 teaspoons light soy sauce
2 teaspoons *sake*
$4^1/_2$ ounces silken bean curd (2-inch x $2^1/_2$-inch
  x $1^1/_2$-inch rectangle), cut in 4 decorative
  shapes
1 spring onion (green part only), sliced
  diagonally

Duck Dumplings:

$^1/_4$ pound finely ground or processed duck or
  chicken breast ($^1/_2$ cup)
1 teaspoon *inaka miso*
$^1/_4$ teaspoon finely grated fresh ginger
1 egg, lightly beaten
1 ounce *yamato* potato, peeled and grated ($^1/_4$
  cup), or an extra 2 teaspoons of cornstarch
1 teaspoon cornstarch

Put basic *dashi* stock in a saucepan, bring to a boil
and add salt, soy sauce and *sake*. Set aside.

Combine all ingredients for **duck dumplings**.
Wet one hand and squeeze a handful of the duck
mixture through your thumb and forefinger onto a
tablespoon and shape into an oblong. Drop into the
gently simmering stock and repeat until all the mixture is used up. Simmer the dumplings for 5 minutes.

Add the bean curd to the stock, reheat, then
serve, dividing the dumplings and bean curd
among 4 lacquer bowls and topping with hot soup.
Garnish with a little of the spring onion and serve
at the beginning of a meal.

STUFFED LOTUS ROOT ◔◔

7 ounces lotus root, peeled
3 hard-boiled eggs, yolks reserved
2 tablespoons white *miso*, strained
1 teaspoon Japanese mustard paste
$^1/_2$ teaspoon sugar
$^1/_2$ teaspoon salt
1 heaped tablespoon white flour
Oil for deep frying

Tempura Batter:

2 egg yolks
2 tablespoons water
1 heaped tablespoon white flour

Boil the lotus root in plenty of water for 5 minutes,
drain and chill. Strain the boiled egg yolks and mix
with *miso*, mustard, sugar and salt. Dust the lotus
root with flour, making sure some goes down the
holes. Fill the lotus root holes with the egg mixture.

Prepare ***tempura* batter** by stirring together the
egg and water, then briefly mixing in the flour. Dip
the filled lotus root in the batter and deep fry in hot
oil. Drain, slice and sprinkle with salt to taste.

HORENSO GOMA AE & MOZUKU

Spinach with Sesame Dressing & Mozuku Seaweed

SPINACH WITH SESAME DRESSING

The spinach is served at room temperature in this simple but tasty appetizer, making it easy to prepare some time in advance. ⏲ ⏲

10 ounces spinach, washed but left whole
5 tablespoons white sesame seeds
5 teaspoons light soy sauce
2 teaspoons sugar
4 teaspoons Basic *Dashi* Stock (page 33)
1 tablespoon very finely shredded toasted laver (*nori*)

Opposite:
*Spinach with
Sesame Dressing
(top and left) and
Mozuku Seaweed
(right).*

Bring a large pan of water to a boil, add the spinach leaves and cook until the leaves soften and darken in color. Pour the spinach into a colander or sieve and cool under running water. Drain, pressing on the spinach with the back of a wooden spoon to extract the water. Put the spinach in a bamboo rolling mat and roll up tightly to squeeze out all the moisture and shape into a roll.

Toast the sesame seeds in a dry pan until golden brown, then crush in a mortar or small blender until coarsely blended. Add the soy sauce, sugar and *dashi* to form a soft paste.

Just before serving, cut the rolled spinach into pieces 1-inch thick and divide among 4 small plates. Top each with a little of the sesame paste and sprinkle with the shredded *nori*.

MOZUKU SEAWEED

The chewy texture of this hair-like seaweed makes it an unusual appetizer. Alternatively, use $3\frac{1}{2}$ ounces each of *wakame* seaweed and sliced cucumber together with the *tosa* vinegar for an excellent appetizer. The rather viscous *yamato* potato provides a striking visual contrast to the seaweed, although if this is not available, use quail eggs or even slices of hard-boiled hen egg. This should be omitted if using *wakame* and cucumber rather than *mozuku* seaweed. ⏲ ⏲

7 ounces *mozuku* seaweed
1 cup *Tosa* Vinegar (page 36)
$1\frac{1}{2}$ ounces *yamato* potato, peeled and finely grated ($\frac{1}{3}$ cup), or 4 hard-boiled quails eggs or 4 slices hard-boiled hen egg
2 teaspoons very finely shredded ginger
4 sprigs of *kinome*, watercress or parsley
Gold powder to garnish (optional)

Soak dried *mozuku* seaweed in water for 2 hours to remove the salt. Put into a sieve and rinse well under hot water. If using water-packed *mozuku*, do not soak, but drain and discard the water. Mix *mozuku* with *yamato* potato or substitute and vinegar and serve garnished with ginger, *kinome* or substitute and gold powder (if using).

KONBU-JIME MATSUMAE AE & SHIRAUO FUBUKI JITATE

Shredded Fish with Kelp & Tempura Whitebait in Soup

Opposite:
Shredded Fish
with Kelp (left)
and Tempura
Whitebait in
Soup (right).

SHREDDED FISH WITH KELP

Two types of dried kelp are used in this appetizer: regular dried kelp is marinated with the fish to add an extra hint of the sea, while salted kelp is mixed with the shredded fish at serving time. ☉ ☉

1/2 pound sea bream fillet, skinned
1 teaspoon salt
1 1/4 ounces dried kelp (*konbu*)
1 heaped tablespoon *mitsuba* or parsley stalks
1/3 ounce salted kelp (*shio-kobu*) (page 28)
1 teaspoon grated fresh horseradish or mixed Japanese horseradish

Cut the bream into slices about 1/4 inch thick and sprinkle with salt. Wipe the dried kelp with a dry towel and cut in half. Place the fish slices on one piece of kelp and top with the second piece to make a sandwich. Cover with a china plate and a weight and refrigerate for 2 days.

Blanch the *mitsuba* or parsley stalks in boiling water for a few seconds, then drain and and chill in cold water. Cut into 3/4-inch lengths.

Cut the squares of salted kelp into fine strips. Remove the sea bream from kelp and mix with *mitsuba* or parsley stalks and the salted kelp. Divide among 4 china bowls and serve with the horseradish on the side.

TEMPURA WHITEBAIT IN SOUP

Fresh whitebait dipped in batter are the highlight of this clear soup. ☉ ☉

1 egg yolk
2 tablespoons *Tempura* Batter (page 37)
1 1/2 ounces fresh whitebait
2 tablespoons white flour
Oil for deep frying
1 pound *daikon*
3 cups Clear Soup (page 34)
Salt to taste
Sprigs of *mitsuba* or parsley
Grated *yuzu* orange or lime or lemon peel

Mix the egg yolk with the *tempura* batter. Shake the white fish and flour together in a plastic bag, then dip into the batter and fry in hot oil until crisp and golden.

Peel and grate the *daikon*, place in a towel and squeeze out all the moisture. Bring the clear soup to a boil and add the grated *daikon*. Season with salt to taste and add the *mitsuba* or parsley. Divide among 4 lacquer soup bowls and add the fried fish just before serving, topped with a little grated peel.

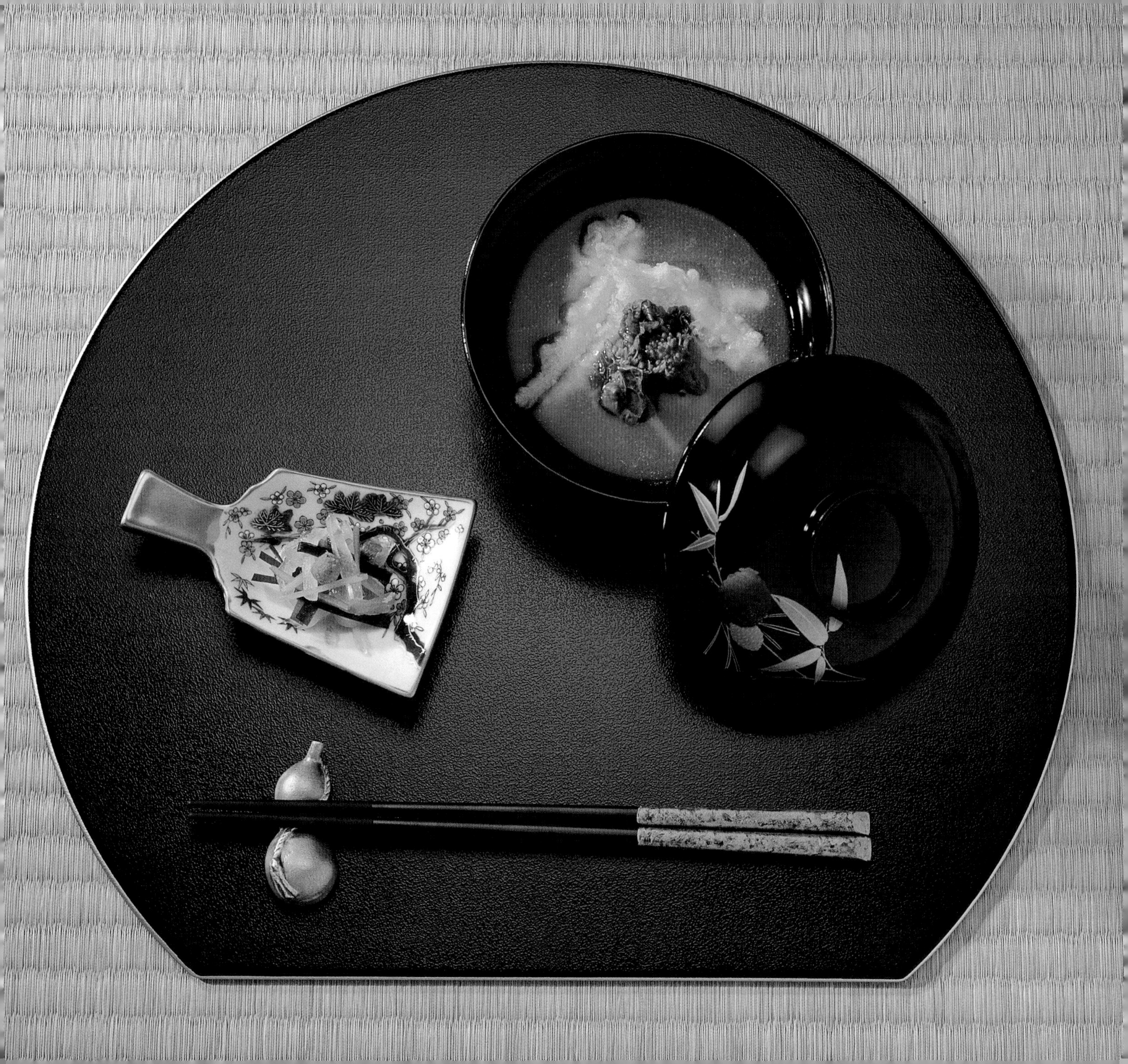

TAMAGO DOFU & GYUNIKU NO TATAKI
Cold Savory Custard & Seared Beef

COLD SAVORY CUSTARD

This chilled custard makes a refreshing summer appetizer, and looks as lovely as it tastes with a sprig of *perilla* or *shiso* flower to garnish. Use any other decorative sprig of tiny edible flowers (flowering basil, for example) as a substitute. ⏱⏱

3 eggs
14 tablespoons Basic *Dashi* Stock (page 33)
2 tablespoons light soy sauce
1 teaspoon *mirin*
4 medium-sized shrimp weighing about 3 ounces, cooked, peeled and tails left on
²⁄₃ cup *Soba Dashi* (2) (page 34)
Grated *yuzu* orange or lime or lemon peel
4 sprigs of *shiso* flower (see above)

Opposite:
Cold Savory
Custard (top right)
and Seared Beef
(center).

Combine the eggs, basic *dashi* stock, soy sauce and *mirin*. Pour through a strainer into a small dish about 4 inches square. Put this into a steamer and steam over boiling water for about 25 minutes, until it sets. Cool, then refrigerate.

Just before serving, cut the savory custard into 4 squares and place each in small glass or china bowl. Place a shrimp on top of each serving, pour in a little of the *soba dashi* and top each serving with grated peel and a *shiso* flower sprig.

SEARED BEEF ⏱⏱

1 pound beef sirloin or rump, in one piece
1 teaspoon salt
2 medium-sized onions
3-inch piece of *daikon*, shredded
4 *ohba* leaves or sprigs of watercress
4 teaspoons finely grated *daikon* mixed with cayenne powder to taste
1 tablespoon finely sliced spring onion
¹⁄₄ cup *Ponzu* Sauce (page 36)

Sprinkle the beef with salt and sear in a very hot pan for a few seconds on each side, just until the color changes. Remove from heat, plunge in iced water for a few second to cool. Dry with a cloth and cut in ¹⁄₄-inch slices.

Peel the onions, halve lengthwise, then cut in thin crosswise slices. Break up the slices with your fingers and put in iced water. Rinse, drain and dry the onion.

To serve, arrange the *daikon* in the center of a plate and surround with the beef. Arrange the *ohba* or watercress in the center, top with the onion, garnish with spring onion and surround with tiny balls of the grated *daikon* and cayenne. Serve with tiny dishes of *ponzu* Sauce as a dip.

NUTA & NAMASU

Tuna, Seaweed and Cucumber & New Year Salad

TUNA, SEAWEED AND CUCUMBER

An excellent combination of raw tuna (the outside merely blanched for a few seconds), crunchy cucumber and chewy *wakame* seaweed. ☻

1/2 pound fresh tuna
1 1/2 heaped tablespoons dried *wakame* seaweed
3 1/2 ounces Japanese cucumbers
1 teaspoon salt
1/3 cup white *miso*
1 1/2 teaspoons sesame paste or smooth peanut
    butter
2 tablespoons plus 2 teaspoons rice vinegar
4 teaspoons sugar
2 teaspoons light soy sauce
2 teaspoons Japanese mustard paste
2 *mioga* buds, cut in fine lengthwise strips
    (optional)

Plunge the tuna in boiling water for 5–10 seconds until the outside starts to turn pinkish white. Remove from the water, chill in iced water for a few seconds, drain again and cut into 2-inch x 3/4-inch pieces about 1/2-inch thick.

Soak the dried *wakame* in hot water until expanded and tender. Drain and set aside. Rub the salt into the outside of the cucumber with your fingers, then slice paper thin. Sprinkle with a generous pinch of salt. Rinse off salt and squeeze out the moisture.

Mix the *miso* with the sesame paste, vinegar, sugar, soy sauce and mustard.

Arrange the tuna, *wakame* and cucumber in a bowl. Garnish with a little of the *miso* mixture and top each serving with a little shredded *mioga*.

NEW YEAR SALAD

This two-colored salad with a sweet vinegar dressing is a traditional New Year dish. ☻

3/4 pound *daikon*
1 large carrot
1 teaspoon salt
5-inch x 3-inch piece dried kelp (*konbu*)
1 cup Sweet Vinegar (page 36)
2 tablespoons shredded *yuzu* orange or lemon
    peel

Cut the *daikon* and carrot into thin slices about 2 inches long. Sprinkle with salt, rubbing it in with your fingers, then rinse the vegetables under running water.

Wipe the dried kelp with a damp cloth, then cut into very fine shreds with a pair of scissors and soak in a little of the sweet vinegar for 20 minutes. Soak the radish and carrot together in the remaining sweet vinegar for 20 minutes. Arrange the radish and carrot on a plate and top with the soaked kelp. Garnish with the peel and serve.

Opposite:
New Year Salad
(left) and Tuna,
Seaweed &
Cucumber Salad
(right).

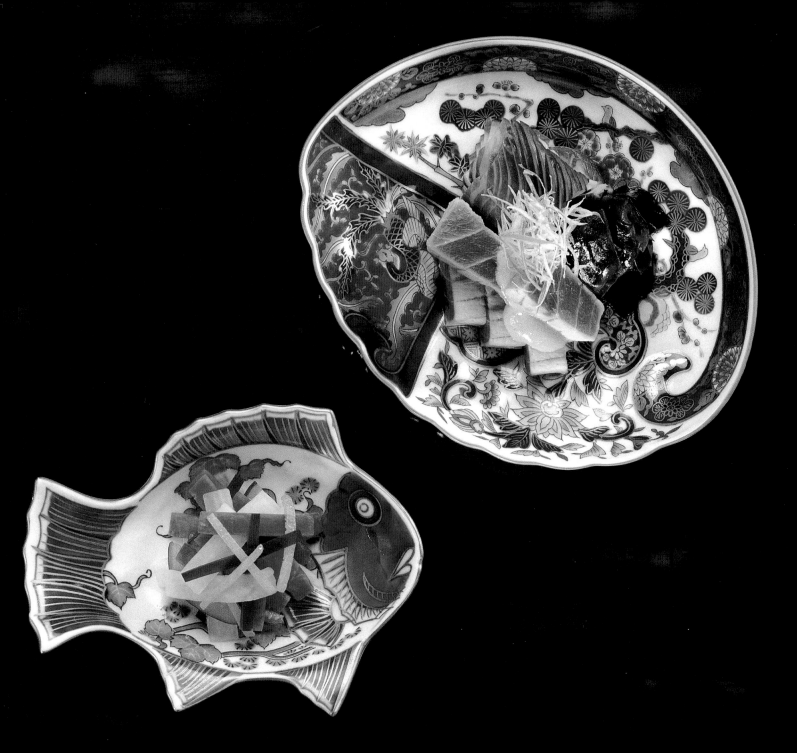

WAKATAKE-NI & NASU MISO-NI
Simmered Bamboo Shoots & Eggplant with Miso

SIMMERED BAMBOO SHOOTS ◐◑

10 ounces fresh or canned bamboo shoots
3 cups rice washing water
2 red chilies
3 cups Basic *Dashi* Stock (page 33)
5 teaspoons *mirin*
5 teaspoons light soy sauce
$^1/_2$ teaspoon salt, or more to taste
$1^1/_2$ tablespoons dry *wakame* seaweed, soaked to soften, cut in $1^1/_2$-inch squares
3 ounces shrimp
1 tablespoon cornstarch
Sprigs of *kinome*, watercress or parsley to garnish

Opposite:
Simmered Bamboo Shoots (top left) and Eggplant with Miso (center).

If using fresh bamboo shoots, simmer in the water used to wash rice with the red chilies for about 2 hours or until soft. Peel the cooked bamboo shoots and keep in running water for 10 minutes. Cut in quarters lengthwise. If using canned bamboo shoots, simmer them in water for 5 minutes only.

Put the boiled fresh or canned bamboo shoots in a saucepan with the *dashi, mirin,* soy sauce and salt and simmer for 15 minutes.

Peel the shrimp, discarding the head and black intestinal vein but leaving on the tail. Slit lengthwise and gently press open in a butterfly shape. Dust the shrimp in cornstarch, shaking off any excess, then plunge in boiling water and simmer just until the cornstarch coating sets. Drain, chill in iced water, drain and set aside.

When the bamboo shoots are cooked, add the *wakame* seaweed to the pan and remove immediately from the heat. Put the pieces of bamboo shoots in 4 bowls and top with shrimp. Pour in the stock and garnish with a sprig of *kinome*. Serve hot.

EGGPLANT WITH MISO

The rather bland flavor of eggplant is transformed by the robust *dengaku miso* sauce with which it is combined. ◐◑

$^3/_4$ pound eggplant
Oil for deep frying
$^3/_4$ cup red *Dengaku Miso*
3 ounces shrimp
1 tablespoon cornstarch
12 snow peas, blanched, chilled and drained

Peel the eggplant and cut into bite-size pieces. Deep fry the eggplant in hot oil for $1^1/_2$ minutes, remove and drain. Mix with the *miso* and set aside.

Peel the shrimp, discarding the head and black intestinal vein but leaving on the tail. Slit lengthwise and gently press open in a butterfly shape. Dust the shrimp in cornstarch, shaking off any excess, then deep fry until cooked. Serve eggplant pieces garnished with shrimp and snow peas.

CHIKUZEN-NI

Vegetables Simmered in Soy Sauce

Any combination of vegetables can be used, according to availability and taste. The amount of stock in this recipe is sufficient for about 1 pound of vegetables. ☯☯

> 3 ounces each of bamboo shoots, carrot, burdock, lotus root, Japanese *sato-imo* or new potatoes, devil's tongue jelly (*konnyaku*)
> 4 fresh *shiitake* mushrooms
> 12 sugar snap peas or snow peas
> 3 ounces chicken
> 2 teaspoons oil

Stock:

> 3 cups Basic *Dashi* Stock (page 33)
> 3 ounces dark soy sauce
> 2 tablespoons sugar
> 2 ounces *sake*

Peel and dice all vegetables and chicken. Separate the devil's tongue jelly (*konnyaku*) with a spoon. Boil the vegetables and devil's tongue jelly, one at a time, in lightly salted water for 5 minutes. Blanch the chicken in boiling water for 20 seconds, drain, chill in iced water and drain again.

Heat the oil and stir fry the vegetables for 2 minutes.

To make the **stock**, put the *dashi* into a pan and add the stir-fried vegetables. Skim the surface and add all other stock ingredients and chicken. Bring to a boil and simmer gently with the pan covered for 20–30 minutes, until the ingredients are cooked.

Arrange the vegetables and chicken in bowls, add a little of the cooking liquid and serve.

YAKI NASU & SUMI-YAKI
Grilled Eggplant & Mixed Grill

GRILLED EGGPLANT

Eggplant grilled over charcoal have an incomparable flavor, enhanced in this recipe by a lightly seasoned stock. ⏱

- **¾ pound eggplant**
- **2 tablespoons Basic *Dashi* Stock (page 33)**
- **2 tablespoons light soy sauce**
- **2 inches ginger root, finely grated**
- **½ cup dried bonito flakes**

Opposite:
Grilled Eggplant (below) and Mixed Grill (top).

Prick the skin of the eggplant in a few places with a toothpick to prevent them from bursting during cooking. Put the eggplant 2 inches above very hot charcoal (or under a very hot gas or electric broiler) and cook, turning frequently until the skin is slightly blackened and the flesh is soft.

Remove from the grill, plunge into cold water, drain and remove the skin. Tear the eggplant apart with a pair of forks or cut lengthwise into ½-inch-wide strips.

Combine the *dashi* and soy sauce. Place the eggplant in a dome shape in 4 serving bowls and add the *dashi*. Top with grated ginger and sprinkle with bonito flakes.

MIXED GRILL

The sweetness of very small whiting or other little white-fleshed fish is excellent, but if these are not available, any white fish fillets can be used in this simple combination of grilled food. ⏱

- **4 Japanese whiting, 2 ounces each, or ½ pound white fish fillets**
- **½ teaspoon salt**
- **4 medium-sized shrimp**
- **4 fresh *shiitake* mushrooms, stems discarded and caps cross cut**
- **8 small Japanese green peppers, or 1 green bell pepper cut in 8 strips**
- **Oil to brush on the peppers**

Accompaniment:
- **½ cup *Ponzu* Sauce (page 36)**
- **2-inch piece *daikon*, finely grated (½ cup)**
- **4 lemon wedges**

Cut Japanese whiting open. Sprinkle whiting or fish fillets with salt and dry in the fresh air for 1 hour. Peel the shrimp and remove the black intestinal tract, but leave on the head and tail. Make a small slit in the sides of each Japanese pepper, if using. Brush the peppers or bell pepper strips with a little oil. Cook all ingredients over charcoal until done. Serve with *ponzu* sauce, *daikon* and a garnish of lemon wedge.

KABOCHA NO NIMONO & INGEN GOMA-AE

Simmered Winter Squash & Green Beans with Sesame

SIMMERED WINTER SQUASH

The best squash to use for this recipe is butternut variety, although any other well-flavored, dense-fleshed winter squash may be used. Winter squash is a very popular vegetable, not only for its sweet taste but for its beautiful bright color. ☉

1 pound winter squash (see above)
3 cups Basic *Dashi* Stock (page 33)
7 tablespoons sugar
$^1/_4$ cup light soy sauce

Opposite:
Simmered Winter Squash (left) and Green Beans with Sesame (right).

Remove the seeds from the squash and scoop out any fibers with a spoon. Cut in 2-inch square pieces, and peel off the skin on the edges of each piece so that the squash holds its shape during cooking. Cut the squash into decorative shapes as desired.

Put the *dashi* and sugar into a pan and bring to a boil. Add the squash and simmer gently for 7–8 minutes. Turn the squash pieces over, add the soy sauce and continue cooking until the squash is tender. Serve warm or at room temperature, with a little of the cooking liquid poured into each bowl.

GREEN BEANS WITH SESAME

This is a perfect combination, although spinach could be substituted for the beans. ☉

2 cups green beans
$^1/_4$ cup sesame paste
$^1/_4$ cup Basic *Dashi* Stock (page 33)
4 teaspoons light soy sauce
5 teaspoons sugar
4 tablespoons finely shredded toasted laver (*nori*)

Boil the beans in lightly salted water until just tender. Drain and cool under cold running water. Cut in $1^1/_2$-inch lengths, on the diagonal if desired.

Mix the sesame paste, *dashi*, light soy sauce and sugar. Put the beans into 4 serving bowls, top each with a spoonful of the sesame dressing and garnish with 1 tablespoon of shredded *nori*.

KINPIRA GOBO & TOFU DENGAKU

Carrots and Burdock & Miso-topped Bean Curd

CARROTS AND BURDOCK ⊘

6 ounces burdock
1 large carrot
$^{1}/_{2}$ cup Basic *Dashi* Stock (page 33)
3 teaspoons sugar
2 tablespoons plus 2 teaspoons light soy sauce
1 tablespoon vegetable oil
1 teaspoon sesame oil
Seven-spice powder (*shichimi*) to taste
1 teaspoon white sesame seeds, toasted in a dry
     pan until golden-brown

Scrape the skin from the burdock with the back of a knife. Cut into matchstick strips 2 inches long and set aside in water. Peel and cut the carrot the same size as the burdock.

Combine the *dashi* and sugar in a pan and heat until the sugar is dissolved. Add the soy sauce and set aside.

Heat the oil in a wok or frying pan and stir-fry the burdock for 1–2 minutes until it is half-cooked. Add the carrots and stir fry until the vegetables are well coated with the oil. Pour in the *dashi* and simmer until the vegetables are cooked. Sprinkle with sesame oil and stir. Put into 4 serving bowls, then sprinkle with a little seven-spice powder and sesame seeds. Serve at room temperature.

MISO-TOPPED BEAN CURD ⊘⊘

2 blocks of bean curd (16–18 ounces)
$^{3}/_{4}$ cup white *Dengaku Miso* (page 37)
6 tablespoons red *dengaku miso* (page 37)
1 teaspoon very finely grated *yuzu* orange or
     lemon peel
$^{1}/_{3}$ cup *kinome*, watercress, parsley leaves or
     spinach leaves

To remove excess moisture from the bean curd, wrap in a clean towel, place between 2 cutting boards and let stand for 20 minutes. Cut the bean-curd into pieces $^{3}/_{4}$ inch thick, 2 inches long and $^{3}/_{4}$ inch wide.

Prepare the three *miso* toppings. For the red topping, put the red *dengaku miso* in a bowl; it needs no further addition. To make the yellow topping, mix 6 tablespoons of the white *dengaku miso* with the grated *yuzu* peel and set aside. To make the green topping, purée the *kinome*, watercress or parsley leaves to obtain a juice and mix with 6 tablespoons white *dengaku miso*. For a stronger green color, use spinach leaves.

Grill the pieces of bean curd until lightly colored on both sides. Spread each piece of bean curd with one of the three colored toppings and return to the grill until they take color. Carefully insert a skewer into each bean curd and serve hot.

TSUKURI MORIAWASE

Assorted Sashimi

A wide variety of seafood is enjoyed raw as *sashimi*, cut in different ways depending upon the texture of each particular ingredient. *Sashimi* is served with a variety of garnishes, condiments and dipping sauces, some sauces being considered more appropriate to certain types of seafood than others. You may decide to serve just one or two types of fish, or a range of several, but whatever variety you choose, be absolutely certain that the fish is spanking fresh. ◷ ◷

4 jumbo shrimp
$^1/_4$ pound scallops
$^1/_2$ teaspoon oil
5 ounces halfbeak fillet or tuna
10 ounces snapper fillet
$^1/_4$ cup shredded *daikon*
4 *shiso* leaves
4 teaspoons Japanese horseradish paste
4 tablespoons *Tosa* Soy Sauce (page 34)

Peel the shrimp, remove the dark intestinal vein but leave on the head and tail for a more attractive appearance. Clean and dry the scallops. Heat the oil in a nonstick pan until moderately hot and sear the scallops for 30 seconds on each side. Remove and set aside.

Scale the fish and remove any small bones. Cut the halfbeak fillet on the diagonal into strips about $^1/_2$ inch wide and $1^1/_4$ inches long. If using tuna, cut into $^3/_4$-inch cubes. The snapper can either be sliced paper thin or cut to resemble a leaf (see photo).

Serve the shrimp, scallops and cut fish arranged decoratively on a rectangular plate. Garnish with *daikon*, *shiso* leaf and horseradish, and serve with bowls of *tosa* soy sauce for dipping.

AKA-GAI SASHIMI & GYU-NIGIRI
Cockle Sashimi & Beef Sushi

COCKLE SASHIMI

Sometimes called bloody clams because of their red entrails, and also known as ark shells, these make an interesting *sashimi*. Other shellfish such as scallops, fan shells, abalone or turban shells can be used as an alternative. ⏱

12 cockles or alternative (see above)
¹/₂ cup shredded *daikon*
4 *ohba* or other large decorative leaves
4 sprigs of *shiso* flowers or alternative garnish
4 heaped teaspoons *benitade* or alfalfa sprouts
4 teaspoons Japanese horseradish paste
4 tablespoons *Tosa* Soy Sauce (page 34)

Opposite:
Beef Sushi (left)
and Cockle
Sashimi (right).

Open the cockles by inserting a knife along the back of the shells. Remove the meat, discarding any hard parts as well as any entrails. Slit each cockle down the center and press open in a butterfly shape. Cut several shallow slits on the outside of the cockle meat and fling it to the cutting board to make it become crunchy in texture. Arrange the shellfish on the shredded radish and garnish with the leaves, *shiso* flowers, *benitade* and horseradish. Serve with side dishes of *tosa* soy sauce.

BEEF SUSHI

It may come as a surprise to learn that raw beef is used as a topping on *sushi* rice in some Japanese restaurants. Unlike the Italian *carpaccio*, the beef is not marinated but gets its flavor from the rice and accompaniments. ⏱

5 ounces prime marbled beef sirloin, very thinly sliced
1 teaspoon crushed garlic
6 tablespoons Vinegared Rice (page 37)
4 tablespoons pickled ginger slices
4 sprigs of *shiso* flower or alternative garnish
4 heaped teaspoons *benitade* or alfalfa sprouts
4 tablespoons light soy sauce

Cut the beef slices into pieces about 2¹/₂ inches long and ³/₄ inch wide. Hold a beef slice in one hand and spread it with a little of the garlic. Wet your other hand and form a heaped tablespoonful of *sushi* rice into an oval. Lay the rice onto the beef and press down slightly so that the beef adheres to the rice.

Arrange on a serving dish and serve garnished with ginger, *shiso* flowers and *benitade*, with side dishes of soy sauce.

KATSUO TATAKI

Seared Bonito with Tangy Dressing

Lightly seared bonito is marinated with tangy seasonings in this refreshing chilled dish, perfect for a hot summer day. ☯☯

Oil to grease pan
3/4 pound bonito fillet, skin left on
1/3 cup spring onion, very finely shredded lengthwise
1 ounce (4-inch piece) ginger root, very finely shredded lengthwise
1–2 cloves garlic, very finely chopped
1/2 lemon, thinly sliced
1/3 cup *Ponzu* Sauce (page 36)
1/4 cup shredded *daikon*
1 heaped tablespoon finely grated daikon mixed with seven-spice powder or cayenne to taste

Heat a lightly greased nonstick frying pan. Put in the bonito fillet, skin side up, and sear just until the outside of the fish turns white. Turn and sear the other side, then soak in iced water for 10–15 seconds to chill. Wipe away any moisture and marinate the whole fillet with half of the spring onion, ginger, garlic, lemon and half of the *ponzu* sauce, patting the fish with the side of a knife to let the sauce penetrate. Chill in the refrigerator for a minimum of 10 minutes. Cut the marinated bonito in 1/2-inch slices.

Arrange the bonito on a bed of *daikon* strips garnished with the remaining sliced spring onion, ginger and garlic on a platter. Arrange the remaining lemon slices and and seasoned grated *daikon* on the side and served either at room temperature or chilled.

BATTERA SUSHI

Vinegared Rice with Kelp

Very fine golden-colored kelp (*shiraita konbu*) is soaked and used to cover this *sushi*, which is rolled in a bamboo mat before being cut. 🕐 🕐

10 ounces mackerel fillets
³/₄ cup salt
Large sheet or 2 sheets golden kelp
  (***shiraita konbu***)
14 tablespoons rice vinegar
³/₄ cup Vinegared Rice (page 37)
1 teaspoon white sesame seeds
4 tablespoons light soy sauce
4 tablespoons pickled ginger slices

Sprinkle the mackerel fillets lightly with salt and refrigerate for 1½ hours. Rinse and pat dry. Soak the golden kelp in water to cover until soft and transparent. Remove any small bones from the mackerel. Place vinegar in a glass or ceramic dish, add the mackerel fillets and refrigerate for 40 minutes. Cut the skin from fish.

Wet a cotton cloth, wring it dry, then place it on a bamboo rolling mat. Put the skin across the cloth and spread the rice evenly over the skin. Top with a fillet of fish, sprinkle with sesame seeds and cover the top with the golden kelp. Start to roll up, helping to shape the contents into a smooth, even roll.

Unroll, cut in ³/₄-inch slices and serve with soy sauce and pickled ginger.

Helpful hint: If preferred, the *sushi* can be pressed into a rectangular container rather than rolled. Place the skin on the bottom and layer it with rice, fish, sesame seeds and golden kelp. Cover and put on a weight to compress the *sushi*. Leave to stand for 15 minutes before cutting.

HOSOMAKI & CHIRASHI-ZUSHI

Rolled Sushi & Sushi Rice with Topping

ROLLED SUSHI

Three different fillings are used in these *nori*-wrapped rolls of vinegared rice: tuna, cucumber and pickled *daikon*, the last available in jars in Japanese stores. ◷ ◷

- **4 large sheets toasted dried laver (*nori*), each about 8 inches x 7 inches**
- **1½ cups Vinegared Rice (page 37)**
- **6 ounces fresh tuna**
- **6 ounces cucumber (½ English cucumber)**
- **6 ounces pickled *daikon* strips**
- **1 teaspoon mixed Japanese horseradish paste**
- **2 tablespoons pickled ginger slices**

Opposite:
Sushi Rice with Topping (center of box) surrounded by Rolled Sushi.

Cut the raw tuna in 4 strips of the same length as the *nori*. Cut the cucumber in quarters lengthwise, remove the seeds and cut into sticks. Cut the *nori* in half. Place the half *nori* sheet on a bamboo rolling mat, with the shiny side down. Top the *nori* with ½ cup of the *sushi* rice, spread evenly on the sheet leaving a border of ½ inch free on the inside of the sheet.

Take a little horseradish paste on your finger and spread it across the rice in the center. Place the tuna across the center of the horseradish and start to roll using the bamboo mat, making sure the *nori* sheet end goes under the rice. Roll the mat up firmly and squeeze gently. Remove the rolled *sushi* from the mat, cut in half and then into three pieces with a wet knife. Repeat the process with a filling of cucumber and again with a filling of pickled radish. Serve garnished with pickled ginger.

SUSHI RICE WITH TOPPING ◷ ◷

- **2½ cups cooked Vinegared Rice (page 37)**
- **1 tablespoon tiny dried fish (optional, see below)**
- **4 tablespoons finely shredded toasted laver (*nori*)**
- **4 eggs, lightly beaten and fried as an omelet and shredded**
- **4 medium-sized cooked shrimp, halved and open butterfly style**
- **3 ounces raw tuna, cut in strips**
- **2 ounces squid, blanched and cut in strips**
- **⅔ ounce grilled eel (available canned or in vacuum packs)**
- **⅓ cup shrimp flakes (page 72)**
- **4 tablespoons pickled ginger slices**
- **4 teaspoons light soy sauce**
- **4 teaspoons mixed Japanese horseradish paste**

Mix the *sushi* rice with dried fish (thread-like dried and cooked silver fish sold in packets). Put the mixture in 4 lacquer bowls or wooden boxes and level the surface. Scatter with seaweed and omelet and place all other ingredients decoratively on top.

NORIMAKI

Mixed Rolled Sushi

Several different ingredients are combined inside a roll of *sushi* rice wrapped in toasted laver (*nori*). ☻ ☻

1¼ ounces grilled eel (available canned or in vacuum packs)
2 ounces cooked shrimp, peeled
2 ounces cucumber (¼ English cucumber)
¼ cup shrimp flakes (see below)
2 eggs, beaten and fried as an omelet
2 sheets of toasted dried laver (*nori*)
1 cup Vinegared Rice (page 37)
4 tablespoons pickled ginger slices
4 tablespoons light soy sauce

Shrimp Flakes:

5 ounces small shrimp, peeled and deveined
1 egg yolk
2½ tablespoons sugar
¼ teaspoon salt
Red food coloring

Prepare the **shrimp flakes** first by rinsing the shrimp in lightly salted water. Drain and then simmer in a little salted water until they change color. Drain, cool and blend in a food processor to make a purée. Tie the shrimp in cheesecloth and leave to soak in water for 1–2 minutes to remove any smell. Drain the shrimp and knead the cheesecloth gently to extract all the moisture.

Put the shrimp in a bowl and add egg yolk, sugar and salt, mixing well. Add just a touch of food coloring diluted in water to make the shrimp a pale pink. Put the shrimp into a nonstick pan and cook over low heat, stirring from time to time, for about 30 minutes or until almost dry. (This can be kept refrigerated for up to 1 week. Packets or jars of prepared shrimp or shrimp flakes are often available in Japanese stores.)

Cut the eel, shrimp, cucumber and omelet into sticks of the same length. Place the *nori* on a bamboo rolling mat and spread half the *sushi* rice on the *nori*, leaving the upper and bottom border free by ½ inch. Sprinkle the rice with half the shrimp flakes. Arrange half the ingredients side by side in a row on the rice. Start to roll using the bamboo mat, making sure the *nori* sheet end goes under the rice. Roll the mat up firmly and squeeze gently. Remove the rolled *sushi* from the mat, cut in half and then into ¾-inch slices with a wet knife. Repeat the process with remaining filling.

Serve garnished with pickled ginger and soy sauce for dipping.

KAREI SHIO-YAKI & HOTATE YUZU KAMA-YAKI

Flat Fish with Salt & Scallops in Yuzu

FLAT FISH WITH SALT

Sprinkling fresh fish liberally with salt before grilling helps keep in the moisture. ⊘⊘

- 1$\frac{1}{3}$ pounds flat fish, such as flounder, sole or pomfret
- 2 tablespoons salt
- Lemon wedge to garnish
- 10-inch piece *daikon*, very finely grated and squeezed to extract moisture

Lotus Root Garnish:

- 2 ounces fresh lotus root, peeled and thinly sliced
- 3 tablespoons Sweet Vinegar (page 36)
- 1 red chili, seeds discarded
- $\frac{1}{3}$ cup *Ponzu* Sauce (page 36)

Opposite:
*Flat Fish with Salt
(top) and Scallops
in Yuzu (below).*

Prepare **lotus root garnish** several hours before it is required. Boil the sliced lotus root in water for 30 seconds, drain and put it in the sweet vinegar. Heat the chili in a dry pan for a few seconds, then add to the vinegar and *ponzu* sauce. Refrigerate.

Clean and scale the fish. Dry with a paper towel and make two deep crosswise incisions on each side. Put a skewer through the tail end of the fish, making it come out in the center and continuing to the head so that the fish has a wave shape. Sprinkle both sides of the fish lightly with salt, then press a liberal amount of salt onto the tail and fins.

Cook the fish over a moderately hot charcoal fire or under a broiler, turning it with the skewer to avoid damaging the skin, until the fish is golden on both sides and cooked through. Serve on a plate garnished with lemon wedge, grated *daikon* and the marinated lotus root.

SCALLOPS IN YUZU ⊘⊘

- 6 ounces fresh scallops, quartered
- $\frac{1}{2}$ cup red *Dengaku Miso* (page 37)
- 4 *yuzu* oranges or mandarins
- 4 white *hime* radishes, or 4-inch piece of *daikon*, quartered
- 4 teaspoons *moro miso* or red *miso*

Mix the scallops with the *dengaku miso*. Cut off the top of each *yuzu* and reserve as a lid. Hollow out the rest of the *yuzu* carefully and fill each with some of the scallop mixture. Set the lid aside and bake the filled *yuzu* in a 350°F oven for 15 minutes.

While the scallops are baking, peel the radish and boil in lightly salted water until soft. Drain, cool in iced water and reserve.

Place a *yuzu* and its lid on each serving dish, garnish with the radish and 1 teaspoon of *miso*.

Helpful hint: Shrimp can be substituted for scallops.

EBI-NI & BANSHU-MUSHI

Shrimp with Sake & Fish with Noodles

SHRIMP WITH SAKE ⊘

12 fresh shrimp (weighing 8–10 ounces)
1 cup Basic *Dashi* Stock (page 33)
$^1/_2$ cup *sake*
2 tablespoons sugar
2 tablespoons light soy sauce
$^3/_4$ inch ginger root, sliced
8 snow peas, blanched in lightly salted water
    and chilled

Opposite:
*Shrimp with Sake
(left) and Fish
with Noodles
(right).*

Trim the whiskers and legs of each shrimp but do not peel. Use a toothpick to remove the intestinal vein at the back of the head. Place the shrimp in a pan with the *dashi*, *sake*, sugar, soy sauce and ginger. Simmer for 3–4 minutes over high heat. Add the snow peas at the last moment. Drain the shrimp and peel, leaving on the head and tail. Arrange on a plate with the snow peas and serve at once.

FISH WITH NOODLES ⊘⊘

8 ounces red snapper fillet
$^1/_2$ teaspoon salt
4 ounces dried fine wheat noodles (*somen*)
4 ounces *shimeji* mushrooms
1 heaped tablespoon very finely grated *daikon*,
    mixed with cayenne powder to taste
$1^1/_2$-inch piece spring onion, very finely shred-
    ded lengthwise

Stock:
1 cup Basic *Dashi* Stock (page 33)
$2^1/_2$ tablespoons *mirin*
$2^1/_2$ tablespoons light soy sauce

Sprinkle the fish with salt, cut in 4 pieces and put on a plate. Cook in a steamer for 5–6 minutes, remove and set aside.

Heat all the **stock** ingredients together in a saucepan and reserve. Divide the noodles in 4 bundles and tie one end of each bundle with cotton thread to prevent the noodles from separating during cooking. Cook the noodles in plenty of boiling water until just cooked, rinse under cold water and drain, leaving the thread still in position.

Place each bundle of noodles in a serving bowl, leaving half of the bundle hanging out. Top each bundle of noodles with a piece of red snapper and fold back the noodles hanging out of the bowl so as to enclose the fish. Cut off the end of the noodles tied with the thread and discard. Add the mushrooms to the bowl and return to the steamer. Cook over rapidly boiling water for 5 minutes.

Remove the fish from the steamer and pour over the hot stock. Garnish each portion with $^1/_2$ tablespoon of grated *daikon* shaped into a ball and sprinkle a little of the spring onion on top.

AMADAI ITO-UNI YAKI

Red Snapper with Sea Urchin Threads

Sea urchin threads, hair-like orange shreds with a delicate flavor, add color and contrast to the fish. They are available frozen in Japanese stores, but could be replaced with sea urchin paste, available in glass jars. ☺ ☺

> **10 ounces red snapper fillet**
> **$\frac{1}{2}$ teaspoon salt**
> **2 teaspoons *sake***
> **2 egg yolks, stirred**
> **Just under 1 ounce sea urchin threads or 2 teaspoons sea urchin paste (see above)**

Garnish:

> **4 small fresh abalone**
> **$\frac{1}{2}$ cup Basic *Dashi* Stock (page 33)**
> **2 teaspoons *sake***
> **2 teaspoons sugar**
> **1 teaspoon dark soy sauce**
> **$\frac{1}{2}$ teaspoon very finely grated ginger root**

Cut the snapper fillet into 4 portions, sprinkle with salt and refrigerate for 2 hours. Skewer each piece of fish on 3 skewers so that it will hold its shape during grilling. Sprinkle the fish with *sake* and grill over charcoal or under a gas or electric broiler at medium temperature for 10 minutes.

During the cooking process, brush the skin of each piece of fish with egg yolk and return to the grill three times. On the fourth time, give a final baste with egg yolk and cover with sea urchin threads and grill for another 30 seconds. If using sea urchin paste, mix it with the egg yolks before the first brushing of the fish.

Place fish on serving platters. Remove the skewers carefully by twisting them slightly.

Prepare the **garnish** by washing the abalone well in hot water, then discard the abalone heads. Remove from the shell and make incisions in the back of each abalone at a distance of $\frac{1}{4}$ inch. Combine the *dashi*, *sake*, sugar and soy sauce in a small saucepan and bring to a boil. Add the ginger and abalone. Simmer very gently for 10 minutes. Remove the abalone and return to the shells to serve as a garnish.

SHIBA-MUSHI & URAJIRO SHIITAKE

Steamed Sea Bass with Vegetables & Shrimp-stuffed Mushrooms

STEAMED SEA BASS WITH VEGETABLES ⏱⏱

10 ounces sea bass fillet, cut in 4 pieces
1 teaspoon salt
2 tablespoons *sake*
$^1/_2$ pound *enoki* or golden (*enokitake*) mushrooms
$^1/_4$ pound *shimeji* mushrooms
$^1/_2$ cup asparagus, cut in1$^1/_4$-inch lengths, blanched in boiling water
1 small carrot, in julienne shreds 1$^1/_4$ inches long, blanched in boiling water
1 spring onion, cut in 1$^1/_4$-inch lengths

Stock:
1$^1/_2$ cups Basic *Dashi* Stock (page 33)
2 tablespoons *mirin*
4 teaspoons light soy sauce
2 teaspoons salt

Sprinkle the fish fillets with salt and marinate for 20 minutes. Sprinkle with *sake*, put in a shallow bowl and steam for 5 minutes.

Discard the hard ends of the *enoki* mushrooms. Discard the stems of the *shimeji* mushrooms and halve crosswise. Boil the mushrooms separately in a little of the *dashi* for the stock. Place the sea bass in 4 serving bowls, arrange the cooked vegetables on top. Combine the **stock** ingredients, heat and pour over the fish. Garnish with spring onions.

SHRIMP-STUFFED MUSHROOMS ⏱⏱

$^3/_4$ pound fresh shrimp, peeled
16 fresh *shiitake* mushrooms, stems discarded
3 tablespoons cornstarch
Oil for deep frying
4 sprigs of watercress or parsley
$^1/_2$ cup *Tempura* Batter (page 37)
2 tablespoons *daikon*, very finely grated and mixed with cayenne to taste

Dipping Sauce:
1 cup Basic *Dashi* Stock (page 33)
4 tablespoons sugar
4 tablespoons dark soy sauce

Chop or process the shrimp to make a smooth paste. Press a little of the shrimp paste into each mushroom, dust the top with a little cornstarch. Deep fry the mushrooms, a few at a time, in hot oil for 2 minutes. Drain and divide among 4 serving plates.

Dip each sprig of watercress or parsley in *tempura* batter and deep fry until the batter is golden brown. Remove, drain and put beside the mushrooms. Garnish each serving with $^1/_2$ tablespoon of the *daikon*. To prepare the **dipping sauce**, combine the *dashi*, sugar and soy sauce, mixing well, and divide among 4 bowls.

Opposite:
Steamed Fish with Turnip (top; no recipe provided) and Steamed Sea Bass with Vegetables (right). Photo of Shrimp-stuffed Mushrooms is on page 84.

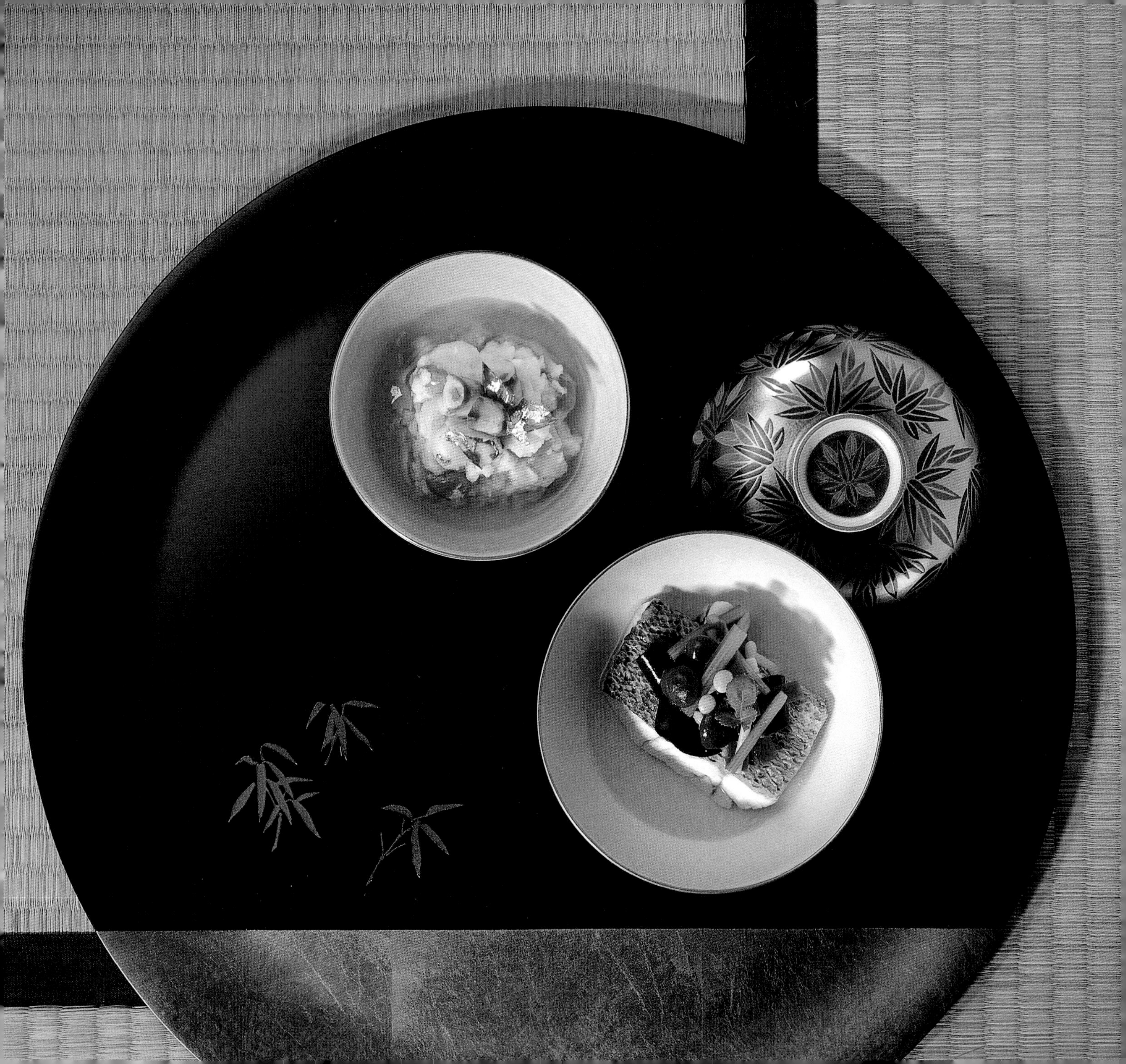

BURI NO NITSUKE & CHAWAN-MUSHI

Simmered Yellowtail & Savory Custard

SIMMERED YELLOWTAIL ☻☻

1 pound yellowtail
10-inch piece *daikon*, in $3/4$-inch slices
$1^1/_2$ cups rice washing water
8 cups water
2 cups *sake*
$3/4$ inch ginger root, sliced
$1/2$ cup sugar
$2/3$ cup dark soy sauce
Sprig of *kinome* or watercress

Opposite:
Simmered
Yellowtail (center)
and Savory
Custard (below).

Cut the yellowtail into four $1^1/_2$-inch-square pieces and blanch in boiling water for 10–20 seconds to remove any strong fish odor. Boil the sliced *daikon* for 15 minutes in water in which rice has been washed. (This water helps the *daikon* remain white.) Drain, chill in iced water and drain again.

Put 8 cups water and *sake* into a large saucepan. Add the yellowtail, cooked *daikon* and sliced ginger. Bring to a boil and simmer for 5 minutes, skimming the surface regularly, then add sugar and simmer for 1 hour until the liquid has reduced by half. Add the soy sauce and continue simmering for another hour, by which time the liquid will have reduced to about $2^1/_2$ cups.

Serve the fish and *daikon* in a large bowl and top with *kinome* or watercress.

SAVORY CUSTARD ☻☻

2 ounces chicken breast, in bite-size pieces
2 teaspoons light soy sauce
$1^1/_2$ ounces baked eel (sold in vacuum packs), cut in 4 pieces
$2/3$ ounces lily root, cleaned and cut in 4 pieces (optional)
4 fresh *shiitake* mushrooms, stems discarded
4 large shrimp, peeled and intestinal veins removed
1 tablespoon ($1^1/_4$-inch lengths) *mitsuba* or parsley stalks
8 gingko nuts, peeled, blanched and thin skins removed
2 large eggs
$3/4$ cup Basic *Dashi* Stock (page 33)
3 teaspoons light soy sauce
Shredded *yuzu* orange or lemon peel to garnish

Sprinkle the chicken with soy sauce. Assemble the eel, lily root, mushrooms, shrimp, *mitsuba* or parsley stalks and gingko nuts.

Break the eggs in a bowl and mix gently with chopsticks to avoid making bubbles. Add the *dashi* stock and soy sauce. Mix well and strain. Divide all the assembled ingredients among 4 individual china bowls or cups with lids and pour in the egg mixture. Steam for 10 minutes over medium heat. Serve garnished with *yuzu* orange or lemon peel.

SAKE NO TSUMIRE-AGE

Salmon Bean Curd Balls

This combination of delicately seasoned salmon and bean curd makes a light and palate-pleasing dish. ⏲ ⏲

- **½ pound salmon fillet, coarsely chopped**
- **9-ounce block bean curd**
- **Handful of *mitsuba* leaves or parsley with stalks attached**
- **2 fresh *shiitake* mushrooms, stems discarded and caps very finely shredded**
- **1¼-inch piece carrot, cut in matchsticks**
- **1 cloud-ear fungus, soaked until swollen and very finely shredded**
- **1 egg, lightly beaten**
- **½ teaspoon salt**
- **2 teaspoons light soy sauce**
- **1 teaspoon sugar**
- **5 teaspoons cornstarch**
- **Oil for deep frying**

Accompaniments:

- **4 tablespoons light soy sauce**
- **2 teaspoons Japanese mustard paste**

Opposite:
Shrimp-stuffed Mushrooms (left) and Salmon Bean Curd Balls (right). Recipe for Shrimp-stuffed Mushrooms is on page 80.

Put the chopped salmon in a bowl. Soak the bean curd in water for 1–2 minutes, drain in a cloth-lined sieve, then squeeze out excess moisture by wrapping the bean curd in the cloth and twisting tightly. Add this to the salmon.

Separate the stalks from the *mitsuba* or parsley and chop finely, keeping the whole leaves aside. Add 1–2 teaspoons of the chopped stems to the salmon and bean curd, then add all other ingredients except oil and **accompaniments**. Mix well and shape into small balls.

Deep fry in hot oil, turning frequently, until golden brown and cooked. Drain and put in individual serving baskets. Spray the *mitsuba* or parsley leaves with a little water, then dip in additional cornstarch. Deep fry in hot oil for a few seconds until the coating sets. Garnish the salmon balls with the fried *mitsuba* and accompany with side dishes, each containing 1 tablespoon of soy sauce with ½ teaspoon of mustard.

HOTATE RINGO KAMA-YAKI & TACHIUO YAHATA-MAKI

Scallops in Apples & Yahata-Style Cutlassfish

SCALLOPS IN APPLES ◑◑

4 red apples
$\frac{1}{2}$ pound scallops, washed and dried
4 fresh *shiitake* mushrooms
4 small Japanese green peppers or $\frac{1}{2}$ green bell
    pepper
1 teaspoon oil
Salt and pepper to taste
6 tablespoons Japanese Mayonnaise (page 37)
2 tablespoons white *miso*
$\frac{1}{2}$ teaspoon grated *yuzu* or lemon peel

Opposite:
*Scallops in Apples
(left) and
Yahata-style
Cutlassfish (right).*

Cut $\frac{1}{2}$ inch from the top of each apple and reserve. Hollow out each apple carefully, leaving $\frac{1}{2}$ inch of flesh inside the sides of the skin and $1\frac{1}{2}$ inches of flesh on the bottom. Place in iced water with a little salt.

Cut the scallops, mushrooms and peppers in $\frac{3}{4}$-inch dice. Heat oil and stir fry the diced mixture until the scallops turn white. Season with salt and pepper and put into a mixing bowl. Combine mayonnaise and *miso* with grated peel, then mix with the stir-fried scallops and vegetables.

Fill each apple with one-quarter of this mixture (keeping the lid aside) and bake at 350°F for 20 minutes. Serve with the lid to one side and garnish with green leaves.

YAHATA-STYLE CUTLASSFISH ◑◑

1 pound Atlantic Cutlassfish
$\frac{1}{2}$ pound burdock
1 cup *Soba Dashi* (2) (page 34)
$\frac{1}{2}$ cup water
4 teaspoons sugar
3 tablespoons Eel Sauce (see Baked Eel,
    page 92)
Sansho powder to taste
4 white *hime* radishes, or 4-inch piece of
    daikon, quartered and boiled in lightly
    salted water until tender
4 teaspoons *moro miso* or red *miso*

Cut fillets into $\frac{1}{2}$-inch-thick strips. Clean the burdock, cut in quarters lengthwise and cut each quarter into 5-inch sticks.

Combine *soba dashi*, water and sugar and bring to a boil. Add the burdock and boil until soft. Drain and cool. Make bundles of 3 sticks of burdock and roll up with strips of the fish. Skewer the bundles and grill under medium heat or over a medium charcoal fire for 10 minutes. Remove and coat the rolls with the eel sauce. Grill, brushing with sauce 3–4 more times until the fish is well coated.

Remove the skewers and cut the rolls into $\frac{3}{4}$-inch pieces. Sprinkle with *sansho* and garnish with the radish and *moro miso*.

EBI AAMONDO-AGE & SHIRAUO KARA-AGE

Deep-fried Shrimp with Almonds & Deep-fried Whitebait

DEEP-FRIED SHRIMP
WITH ALMONDS

An excellent modern Japanese dish using almonds rather than more traditional broken noodles for a crunchy exterior. ⊘ ⊘

12 fresh shrimp (about 8 ounces)
2 tablespoons white flour
$\frac{1}{2}$ cup *Tempura Batter* (page 37)
$2\frac{1}{3}$ cups slivered almonds
Oil for deep frying
4 fresh *shiitake* mushrooms, stalks discarded
   and caps cross cut
8 small Japanese green peppers, or 1 green bell
   pepper, cut in strips
1 cup *Tempura Dashi* (page 34)
4 tablespoons finely grated white *daikon*
Seven-spice powder (*shichimi*), to taste

Trim the whiskers and legs of the shrimp with scissors. Peel the body section, but leave on the head and the tail. Remove the dark intestinal vein with a toothpick. Make two or three incisions on the underside of each shrimp to prevent it from curling. Pat dry and dust with flour. Dip each shrimp into the *tempura* batter and then press into the almonds to coat well. Deep fry the shrimp in hot oil until golden brown. Drain and set aside.

Dust the *shiitake* mushrooms and green peppers in flour, dip in *tempura* batter and deep fry.

Arrange the fried shrimp, mushrooms and green peppers on 4 plates. Serve with small bowls of *tempura dashi* for dipping and *daikon*. Each diner sprinkles his portion with seven-spice powder to taste.

Helpful hint: 3 cups of shredded sweet potato, tossed in 2 tablespoons of flour, can be substituted for the almonds. Dust the shrimp with a little cornstarch, then dip in lightly beaten egg white rather than *tempura* batter before pressing into the sweet potato.

DEEP-FRIED WHITEBAIT ⊘

1 pound fresh whitebait
4 tablespoons cornstarch
Oil for deep frying
Salt to taste
1 lemon, cut in wedges

Wash and dry the whitebait. Toss in cornstarch and shake in a colander or sieve to remove excess. Deep fry a handful at a time in very hot oil until crisp and golden brown. Drain and sprinkle with salt just before serving, garnished with lemon wedges.

*Opposite:
Deep-fried Shrimp
with Almonds
(top right) and
Deep-fried
Whitebait (below).*

KONBU-YAKI & MANAGATSUO SAIKYO-YAKI
Kelp-grilled Tuna & Saikyo-style Pomfret

KELP-GRILLED TUNA

Strips of dried kelp (*konbu*) are fashioned into little "boats" which hold the seasoned tuna during baking, adding flavor as well as an unusual appearance to this tasty fish dish. ❷ ❷

3 ounces dried kelp (**konbu**)
10 ounces tuna fillet, chopped coarsely
10 spring onions, finely sliced
1¹/₂ inches ginger root, finely shredded
³/₄ cup white *Dengaku Miso* (page 37)
8 small Japanese green peppers, sliced, or
    1 green bell pepper cut in ³/₄-inch dice

Cut the kelp into 4 strips each 6 inches x 3 inches. Soak in water until soft, drain and pat dry. Cut 2 narrow strips from each piece of the kelp to use as strings. Tie the ends of each piece of kelp so it resembles a boat.

Combine the tuna, spring onion, ginger, *miso* and half the chopped pepper, mixing well. Put one quarter of the tuna mixture in the center of each kelp "boat" and top with the remaining green peppers. Bake in a 350°F oven for 15 minutes. If liked, heat some small pebbles in the oven for 10 minutes and place on each serving plate. Put a tuna-filled kelp "boat" on the top of each and serve hot.

SAIKYO-STYLE POMFRET

You'll need to begin preparing this dish 3 days in advance, as the fish fillets should be marinated for this length of time before being grilled. ❷ ❷

10-ounce pomfret fillet
1³/₄ cups white *miso*
¹/₂ cup *sake*
3 tablespoons sugar
3 tablespoons *mirin*
4 pickled turnips or 3¹/₂-inch piece *daikon*,
    finely grated and squeezed to extract
    moisture

Cut the pomfret fillet into 4 pieces. Combine *miso*, *sake* and sugar in a bowl. Add the pomfret fillets and mix so that they are well coated. Marinate in the refrigerator for 3 days.

Remove the fillets and scrape off all the *miso*. Cut a shallow cross in each fillet and thread each fillet with 3 skewers, so they will hold their shape and be easy to turn during grilling. Broil under low heat for about 20 minutes, until the fish is cooked. Brush the skin side of the fillet with *mirin* and put back under the broiler until it becomes shiny.

Serve each fillet on a dish garnished with a pickled turnip (available in jars) or grated *daikon*.

Opposite:
Kelp-grilled Tuna (right) and Saikyo-style Pomfret (left).

UNAGI KABA-YAKI & HAMAGURI NO KOGANE-YAKI

Baked Eel & Clams with Mushrooms

BAKED EEL ♨♨♨

1¼ pounds fresh eel
4 pickled young ginger shoots
1 teaspoon *sansho* powder

Eel Sauce:

   3 tablespoons *sake*
   2 tablespoons *mirin*
   2 tablespoons light soy sauce
   4 teaspoons sugar
   Eel bones (see below)

Opposite:
Baked Eel (right of plate) and Clams with Mushrooms (left).

Stick an ice pick through the head of eel to fix it to the cutting board. Make a cut from the base of the neck toward the tail, keeping the edge of the knife on the backbone. Open the eel and place the knife on the fillet lying on the cutting board. Cut towards the tail to remove the backbone and reserve the bone for use in the eel sauce. Discard the internal organs and wash the eel fillets in water. Cut off the the tail and the fins. Skewer the eel with 5 skewers at an equal distance from the head to the tail.

Prepare the **eel sauce** by washing the reserved eel bone and grilling until it turns whitish. Put in a pan with all other sauce ingredients and bring to a boil. Skim the surface and continuing simmering until the sauce has reduced by half. Set aside.

Place the skewered eel on a charcoal grill or under a gas or electric broiler, meat side facing the heat. Grill for 3 minutes and turn so that the skin faces the heat. Grill for another 3 minutes.

Brush the eel with the prepared eel sauce and grill each side for a little over 1 minute. Brush and return to the grill for another minute. Repeat another couple of times, then cut the eel into 4-inch pieces and arrange on a platter, garnished with the pickled ginger shoots. Sprinkle with sansho powder.

CLAMS WITH MUSHROOMS ♨♨

8 large clams
4 fresh *shiitake* mushrooms, stems discarded and caps cut in 4
5 tablespoons Japanese Mayonnaise (page 37)
2½ tablespoons white *miso*
1 teaspoon finely rated *yuzu* orange or lemon peel

Boil the clams in a little salted water and remove immediately when the shells open. Drain and remove the meat from each clam, keeping the shell. Cut each clam in half. Put 1 piece of *shiitake* mushroom and 2 clam pieces into each reserved shell. Mix the mayonnaise, *miso* and *yuzu* peel together and top each clam shell with about 2 teaspoons of the mixture. Grill under low heat for 2 minutes, then serve.

YAKITORI

Mixed Chicken and Vegetable Skewers

Skewers of grilled chicken and vegetables are very popular both in Japan and abroad. ☻ ☻ ☻

60 bamboo skewers
10 ounces boneless chicken thigh, cut in
   ³/₄-inch cubes
2 spring onions, cut in 1¹/₄-inch lengths
4 ounces chicken livers, halved
9 fresh *shiitake* mushrooms, stems discarded
   and caps halved
18 small green Japanese peppers, or 2 large
   green bell peppers cut in 18 strips
6 green asparagus, cut in 1¹/₄-inch lengths
Oil to baste
1 cup Chicken *Yakitori* Sauce (page 35)

Chicken Balls:

10 ounces ground minced chicken breast
2 teaspoons sugar
2 teaspoons light soy sauce
1 teaspoon ginger juice (page 25)
1 egg, lightly beaten
2 teaspoons bread crumbs
2 teaspoons white flour
4 cups Basic *Dashi* Stock (page 33)
3 tablespoons *sake*

Condiments:

Seven-spice powder (*shichimi*)
Mixed chili powder (*shichimi togarashi*)
***Sansho* powder**
1 lemon, cut in wedges

Soak the bamboo skewers in water for 1 hour to prevent them from burning.

Prepare the **chicken balls** by combining the ground chicken with sugar, soy sauce, ginger juice, egg, bread crumbs and flour, mixing well. Bring the *dashi* and *sake* to a boil. Shape the chicken mixture into small balls by putting some into your palm and squeezing out a ball about ³/₄-inch in diameter through your thumb and forefinger. Drop into the simmering *dashi*, a few at a time, and simmer until they change color. Drain and thread onto skewers.

Alternate the pieces of chicken thigh and onions on skewers and set aside. Thread the chicken livers on 6 skewers and set aside. Thread the vegetables onto skewers. Brush the vegetables lightly with oil to prevent them from drying out during cooking.

Heat a charcoal barbecue or grill and cook the prepared skewers a few at a time. When the chicken balls, chicken livers and chicken and spring onion skewers are half cooked, brush with *yakitori* sauce and return to the grill briefly; brush the skewers another couple of times while cooking, but take care not to overcook the food.

Serve with the range of condiments.

TORI NO MATSUKAZE & TORI TO ASUPARA KARASHI-AE

Chicken Loaf & Chicken with Asparagus

CHICKEN LOAF

Tiny poppy seeds scattered over the top of this seasoned chicken loaf are supposedly reminiscent of sand on a beach, which is perhaps why the dish is known as "Wind in the Pines." ◷◷

$^3/_4$ pound ground chicken
2 eggs, lightly beaten
$^3/_4$ inch ginger root, very finely chopped
2 tablespoons red *miso*
2 teaspoons *sake*
2 teaspoons dark soy sauce
2 tablespoons sugar
2 teaspoons white flour
1 tablespoon white poppy seeds

Opposite: Chicken Loaf (center) and Chicken with Asparagus (right).

Blend the chicken in a food processor to make a paste, or grind a second time. Add all other ingredients except poppy seeds and process until well mixed, or mix with a wooden spoon.

Grease an 8-inch square baking pan and line with baking paper or oiled foil. Put in the chicken mixture, spreading evenly, then sprinkle with the poppy seeds. Set in a pan half-filled with water and bake in a 350°F oven for about 30 minutes, until the center is firm.

Remove from oven and lift out the baking paper or foil with the loaf on it. Cut the loaf into rectangles or fan shapes. Serve at room temperature.

CHICKEN WITH ASPARAGUS

This quickly and easily prepared dish is a combination of white chicken with bright green asparagus and creamy Japanese mayonnaise. ◷

14–16 ounces chicken breast
$^1/_4$ **teaspoon salt**
8 fresh asparagus spears
4 tablespoons Japanese Mayonnaise (page 37)
2 teaspoons prepared Japanese mustard
Pinch of salt
Sprinkle of white pepper

Cut the chicken into strips $^1/_2$ inch wide and blanch in boiling water until the chicken is just cooked. Drain and plunge into iced water until it is cool enough to handle. Tear or cut the cooled chicken into $1^1/_4$-inch lengths and leave to cool.

Cut the asparagus spears into $1^1/_4$-inch lengths and cook in lightly salted boiling water until just tender. Drain, plunge into iced water for a few seconds, drain and allow to cool. Combine the Japanese mayonnaise with mustard, salt and pepper, mixing well.

Just before serving, divide the chicken and asparagus pieces among 4 bowls and put a spoonful of the prepared sauce on the side of each.

KAMO JIBU-NI

Simmered Duck with Japanese Potato

The Japanese believe that duck is too rich and fatty to be eaten frequently; duck breast, the leanest part of the bird, takes on an excellent flavor when simmered in stock and served with Japanese *sato-imo* potatoes and bright green rape blossom or broccoli. ✆ ✆

10 ounces duck breast
2 tablespoons cornstarch
1¹/₂ cups Basic *Dashi* Stock (page 33)
¹/₂ cup soy sauce
¹/₂ cup *mirin*
3 tablespoons plus 1 teaspoon sugar
4 teaspoons Japanese horseradish paste

Sato-imo Potato:
³/₄ pound *sato-imo* potato or new potatoes
4 cups rice washing water
4 cups Basic *Dashi* Stock (page 33)
3 tablespoons plus 1 teaspoon sugar
¹/₂ teaspoon salt
4 teaspoons light soy sauce
2 tablespoons shredded orange or lemon peel

Rape Blossom:
**2 ounces rape blossom or broccoli de rabe
    (stems discarded)**
¹/₃ cup Basic *Dashi* Stock
2 teaspoons light soy sauce
1 teaspoon *mirin*
¹/₂ teaspoon salt

Cut the duck into pieces about ¹/₂ inch thick and 1¹/₂ inches square. Cut a few incisions into the fat. Dust the duck pieces with cornstarch and set aside. Bring the stock, soy sauce and *mirin* to a boil, add the duck and simmer gently until cooked. Arrange the duck pieces in 4 bowls and garnish each portion with a spoonful of horseradish.

Peel the **sato-imo potatoes**, cut a very thin slice off the top and bottom and cut the sides of each potato to make a hexagonal shape. Simmer the potatoes in the water used for washing rice (or plain water) until just tender. If using new potatoes, deep fry in oil until they just take color, then drain and simmer in rice water as for *sato-imo* potatoes. Drain the simmered potatoes and add the *dashi* to the pan. Bring to a boil, add sugar, salt and soy sauce and simmer the potatoes for 5 minutes. Put the potatoes into 4 serving bowls, add a little of the cooking liquid and top with the strips of orange or lemon peel.

Simmer the **rape blossom** in lightly salted boiling water until just cooked. Drain, cool briefly in iced water and drain again. Put the *dashi* into a pan and bring to a boil. Add soy sauce, *mirin* and salt and remove from the heat. Put the rape blossoms in this stock and let it stand for 30 seconds before draining and adding to the duck as a garnish.

TORINIKU NO BAINIKU AGE & TEBASAKI TO SATO-IMO

Chicken Rolls with Sour Plums & Braised Chicken Wings

CHICKEN ROLLS WITH SOUR PLUMS

The salty sour plums (*umeboshi*) so popular in Japan make a surprise filling in these chicken rolls, which are decoratively wrapped either with a *shiso* leaf or piece of *nori* seaweed. ① ①

Opposite: Chicken Rolls with Sour Plums (top left) and Braised Chicken Wings (below right).

12 ounces chicken breast
2 sour plums (*umeboshi*)
$^{1}/_{2}$ teaspoon salt
1 sheet of toasted laver (*nori*), about 8 inches x 7 inches
8 *shiso* leaves
2 tablespoons cornstarch blended with a little water
Oil for deep frying
1 tablespoon cornstarch
4 wedges of orange or lemon to garnish

Cut the chicken breast into pieces $2^{1}/_{2}$ inches x $^{1}/_{2}$ inch and make a small pocket halfway down, taking care not to cut right through the flesh. Remove the stone from the plums and use a spoon to break it into tiny pieces no bigger than your smallest fingernail. Stuff this piece of sour plum into the pocket cut in the chicken. Sprinkle the chicken with salt.

Cut the *nori* into strips about $1^{1}/_{4}$ inches wide. Wrap 8 of the chicken rolls with a *shiso* leaf, sealing the ends with a little of the blended cornstarch. Wrap the remaining chicken rolls with strips of *nori*

and seal the ends with the blended cornstarch.

Heat oil for deep frying. Dust the chicken rolls with cornstarch and deep fry, a few at a time, for 4–5 minutes or until golden brown and cooked. Serve hot, garnished with wedges of orange or lemon.

BRAISED CHICKEN WINGS ① ①

1 pound chicken wings
4 teaspoons *sake*
1 tablespoon oil
$^{3}/_{4}$ inch ginger root, sliced
12 spring onions, cut in 2-inch lengths
$^{3}/_{4}$ pound *sato-imo* or new potatoes, peeled
2 teaspoons sugar
3 tablespoons plus 1 teaspoon dark soy sauce
12 snow peas, blanched in lightly salted water
4 strips of orange or lemon peel

Marinate chicken wings in *sake* for 30 minutes. Heat the oil and stir fry the chicken wings until they change color. Add ginger, spring onions and just enough water to just cover the chicken. Cover the pan and simmer for 10–15 minutes, then add the potatoes, sugar and soy sauce. Simmer for about 30 minutes until the potatoes are soft.

Divide the chicken wings and potatoes among 4 bowls and garnish each portion with 3 snow peas and a strip of orange or lemon peel.

KATSUDON & BUTANIKU SHOGA-YAKI
Pork Cutlets on Rice & Pork with Ginger

PORK CUTLETS ON RICE ◑ ◑

6–8 cups hot cooked rice
2 medium-sized onions, sliced
1 cup Basic *Dashi* Stock (page 33)
$1/3$ cup *mirin*
$1/3$ cup thick soy sauce
4 teaspoons sugar
4 sprigs of *mitsuba* or parsley with long stems
4 eggs

Pork Cutlets:

1 pound pork loin
Sprinkle of salt and pepper
2 tablespoons white flour
1 egg, lightly beaten
2 cups bread crumbs
Oil for deep frying

Opposite:
Pork Cutlets on Rice (top) and Pork with Ginger (below left).

Prepare the **pork cutlets** first by cutting the pork loin into 4 steaks, making incisions along the fatty edge to prevent it from curling during frying. Season the meat lightly with salt and pepper, dust with flour on both sides, dip in beaten egg and then press into bread crumbs. Deep fry the crumbed pork until golden brown and cooked. Drain and keep aside.

Divide the rice among 4 large bowls. Put the onion, *dashi*, *mirin*, soy sauce and sugar in a pan and simmer until the onion is tender. Put one-quarter of this mixture into a small pan, place one cooked pork cutlet on top, add one-quarter of the *mitsuba* or parsley and pour the beaten egg over the top. Simmer for just a moment, until the eggs are just cooked but still runny; they must not be overcooked so that they become firm and dry. Top one portion of rice with this mixture. Repeat for the remaining three pork cutlets and serve with a side dish of pickles.

PORK WITH GINGER ◑

1 pound pork loin, sliced
4 teaspoons ginger juice (page 25)
3 tablespoons light soy sauce
3 tablespoons *sake*
2 medium-sized onions
2 teaspoons vegetable oil
$1/2$ pound cabbage cut in $1^1/2$-inch squares
   (about 3 cups)
1 cup cubed green bell pepper ($1^1/2$-inch
   squares)

Cut pork slices into $1^1/2$-inch cubes and set aside. Mix ginger juice, soy sauce and *sake* and keep aside. Cut onions in half lengthwise and then cut crosswise in $1/2$-inch slices.

Heat the oil in a frying pan or wok and stir fry the pork until it changes color. Add the cabbage, pepper and onion and continue stir frying until the vegetables and pork are cooked. Pour in the prepared seasoning, mix well and serve hot.

RENKON HASAMI AGE

Lotus Root, Pork and Eggplant Slices

This is rather like a sandwich with a filling of seasoned ground pork between slices of lotus root or eggplant. The "sandwich" is then dipped in a *tempura* batter and deep fried. The pork filling can be prepared in advance if desired. ☺ ☻

10 ounces lotus root, peeled and cut in $\frac{1}{2}$-inch slices and kept in water
2 tablespoons white flour
$\frac{1}{2}$ pound eggplant, cut in $\frac{1}{2}$-inch slices
Oil for deep frying
Salt and pepper to taste
2 teaspoons Japanese mustard paste

Pork Filling:
$\frac{1}{2}$ pound ground pork
$\frac{1}{4}$ cup finely chopped onion
2 teaspoons cornstarch
1 egg, lightly beaten
1 teaspoon dark soy sauce

Tempura Batter:
2 egg yolks
1 cup water
$1\frac{3}{4}$ cups white flour

Prepare **pork filling** by combining all ingredients and mixing well.

Just before the dish is required, dry the lotus root slices well and dust both sides with a little of the flour. Place some of the pork filling on the lotus root and top with another slice of root. Repeat this process for the slices of eggplant.

Prepare the ***tempura* batter** by mixing the egg and water, stirring in the flour quickly and leaving any lumps in the batter. Dip the pork-filled vegetable slices in the batter and deep fry in hot oil until golden brown. Sprinkle with a little salt and pepper and serve on a plate with a dab of Japanese mustard.

Opposite:
Lotus Root, Pork and Eggplant Slices (left) and Sirloin Steak Teriyaki (right). Recipe for Sirloin Steak Teriyaki is on page 106.

Beef Grilled on Hoba Leaf & Sirloin Steak Teriyaki

BEEF GRILLED ON HOBA LEAF

Large *hoba* leaves make an attractive cooking container for this mixture of seasoned beef. ◴

- 4 *hoba* leaves or rectangles of aluminum foil about 6 inches x 3 inches
- 4 fresh *shiitake* mushrooms, quartered
- 1 teaspoon oil
- 8 ounces beef tenderloin, cut in $^1/_2$-inch dice
- 1 heaped tablespoon finely sliced spring onion
- $^3/_4$ inch ginger root, very finely minced
- $^3/_4$ cup *Hoba Miso* (page 37)

Opposite:
Grilled Beef on Hoba Leaf. Photo of Sirloin Steak Teriyaki is on page 105.

Soak the *hoba* leaves in cold water for 1 hour to prevent them from burning during cooking. Stir fry the *shiitake* mushrooms in oil for about 30 seconds, then transfer to a bowl and combine with beef, spring onion, ginger and *hoba miso*. Divide the meat into 4 portions and place each one in the center of a *hoba* leaf or on a piece of foil. Place under a hot broiler and cook for about 5 minutes or until the meat is cooked to taste. Serve immediately.

SIRLOIN STEAK TERIYAKI ◔◴

- $1^1/_3$ pounds sirloin steak, cut in $1^1/_4$-inch cubes
- 8 small Japanese green peppers, or 1 large green bell pepper cut in 8 strips
- 1 teaspoon oil
- 2 cups bean sprouts
- 1 cup oyster mushrooms, cut in $^1/_4$-inch slices

Teriyaki Sauce:
- 1 cup dark soy sauce
- 1 cup *sake*
- $1^1/_4$ cups *mirin*
- $2^1/_2$ tablespoons sugar

Prepare the **teriyaki sauce** first by combining all ingredients in a saucepan and bringing to a boil over medium heat. Simmer until the sauce is reduced to just over 1 cup.

Put the cubes of steak on skewers and grill until about half-cooked. Brush with the *teriyaki* sauce and return to the grill for another 30 seconds or so. Brush again, cook a little longer, then give the steak a final brushing and cook for another 30 seconds or so.

If using Japanese peppers, make a small slit in the side of each. Thread the Japanese peppers or bell pepper strips onto skewers and grill until done.

Heat the oil and stir fry the bean sprouts and mushrooms until just cooked. Serve the vegetables as a garnish for the steak, which should be removed from the skewers before serving.

SUKIYAKI

Beef with Vegetables

Although this is one of the most popular Japanese dishes abroad, *sukiyaki* became known in Japan only around the turn of the century, when the Japanese began eating beef (previously proscribed by Buddhist law). There are two styles of cooking this mixture of meat, vegetables, bean curd and noodles: the Osaka style involves cooking the sauce in the pan at the table with each new addition of ingredients, whereas the easier Tokyo style prepares the sauce in advance, as for this recipe. ⊘ ⊘

$1^1/_4$ pounds prime sirloin beef, sliced
3 small onions, cut crosswise in $^1/_4$-inch slices
5 cups spring onions, diagonally sliced in $^3/_4$-inch pieces
2 cups edible chrysanthemum leaves, cut in 3-inch pieces
2 ounces fresh *shiitake* mushrooms, stems discarded and caps cross cut
$^1/_4$ pound golden or *enoki* (*enokitake*) mushrooms, hard part of stems discarded
$^1/_4$ pound burdock, shaved thinly (optional)
$^3/_4$ pound *shirataki konnyaku* or wheat noodles (*udon*), boiled until just cooked and drained
1 piece grilled bean curd (*yakidofu*), cut in small pieces
8 small baked gluten cakes (*fu*) or 1 cake cotton bean curd, cubed
4 tablespoons ($1^1/_2$ ounces) beef fat (suet)
4 eggs

Sauce:
$^3/_4$ cup light soy sauce
$^2/_3$ cup *mirin*
$^2/_3$ cup *sake*
$^1/_2$ cup sugar

Arrange the beef, vegetables, noodles and both types of bean curd on a platter. Keep the beef fat on a small dish to use for greasing the cooking pan. Put the eggs into individual bowls for dipping the cooked ingredients later.

Prepare the **sauce** by putting all ingredients into a pan. Bring to a boil, remove from heat and pour the sauce into a jug.

When it is time to eat the *sukiyaki*, put the beef fat in a heavy deep frying pan and heat gently so that is melts and spreads over the whole surface of the pan. Discard the fat. Add a little of the sliced beef and vegetables, pour on a little of the prepared sauce and simmer. When the ingredients are cooked, each person helps themselves to whatever they fancy, dipping each morsel in the egg (lightly stirred with the chopsticks) before eating.

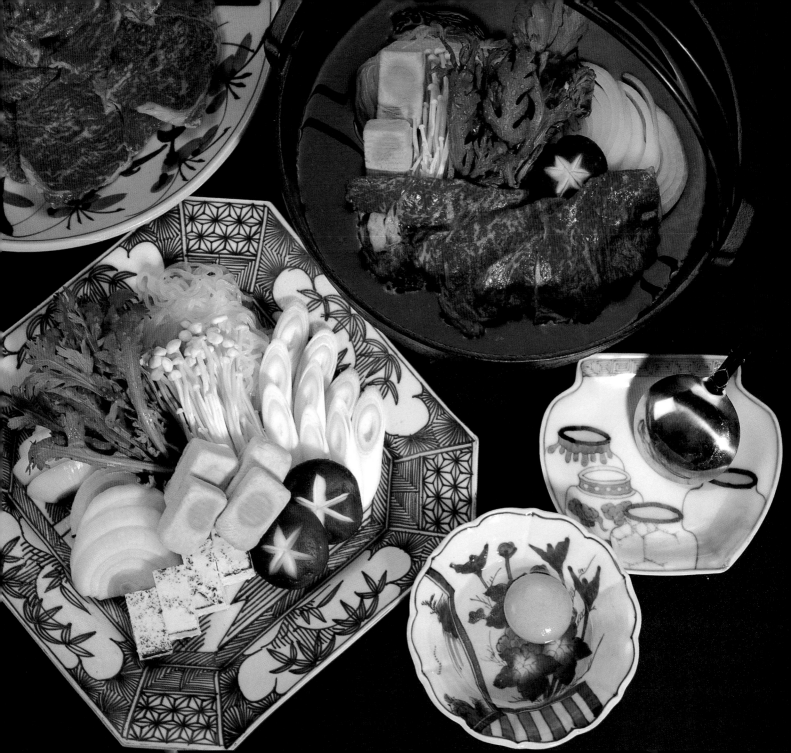

DOTENABE

Oyster and Miso Hotpot

The method of lining the casserole with a layer of *miso* has given rise to the name of this hotpot from Hiroshima, "sand bank." ② ②

1½ pounds oysters in the shell
3½-inch piece *daikon*, grated (³⁄₄ cup)
1½ pounds long white Chinese (Napa) cabbage, 1¼-inch squares
4 ounces edible chrysanthemum leaves, hard parts of stems discarded
12 inches *daikon*, cut in ¼-inch slices and blanched
2 medium-sized carrots, cut in ¼-inch slices and blanched
3 ounces *shiitake* mushrooms
2 cups spring onions
8 ounces golden or *enoki* (*enokitake*) mushrooms
1 pound silken bean curd, cubed
¼ cup *inaka miso*
10 tablespoons white strained *miso*
6 cups Basic *Dashi* Stock (page 33)

Open the oysters and remove from the shell. Mix the grated *daikon* gently by hand with the oysters to remove any dirt. Clean by shaking the colander in salted water. Drain.

Arrange the prepared vegetables, bean curd and oysters on a platter. Mix the two types of *miso* together and spread a layer about ¼ inch thick over the side of a heatproof casserole dish. Bring the *dashi* to a boil and put into the casserole set over a fire in the center of the table. Add the ingredients little by little into the boiling stock and eat. Each person mixes a little *miso* into the stock from the edges of the casserole by brushing it with the morsel of food before eating it.

SHABU-SHABU

Japanese One-pot

An assortment of beef, vegetables and noodles are cooked at the table in a type of fondue generally known as a steamboat or Mongolian hotpot. ☯ ☯

- 1¼ pounds prime sirloin beef, cut in paper-thin slices
- 1 pound long white Chinese (Napa) cabbage
- 10 ounces edible chrysanthemum leaves, hard part of stems discarded
- 8 fresh *shiitake* mushrooms, stems discarded and caps cross cut
- 8 ounces golden or *enoki* (*enokitake*) mushrooms, hard end of stems removed
- 2 cups spring onions, diagonally sliced in ³⁄₄-inch pieces
- 3½ ounces cellophane noodles, soaked in water until transparent
- 6 ounces silken bean curd, cubed

Stock:
- 5-inch x 3-inch piece dried kelp (*konbu*)
- 8 cups water
- 2 teaspoons salt

Accompaniments:
- 1 cup Sesame Dipping Sauce (page 35)
- 1 cup *Ponzu* Sauce (page 36)
- 4 tablespoons finely sliced spring onion
- 4 tablespoons finely grated *daikon* mixed with cayenne to taste

Arrange the beef slices on a plate. Cut the cabbage into 1½-inch squares. Cut out the hard part of the stalk and slice into threads. Arrange the cabbage and all other ingredients on a platter.

To prepare the **accompaniments**, put the sesame sauce into 4 separate bowls. Do the same for the *ponzu* sauce. Put 1 tablespoon each of the spring onion and grated *daikon* onto 4 separate dishes. Give each diner a bowl of sesame dressing, a bowl of *ponzu* and a dish of spring onion with radish.

To prepare the **stock**, wipe the kelp lightly with a damp cloth to clean. Slash in a few places with scissors to release the flavor. Put water and kelp into a saucepan and bring to a boil. Remove the kelp immediately when the stock reaches the boiling point. Reduce the heat and simmer for 2–3 minutes. Add the salt.

Pour the stock into the steamboat and bring to a boil. Each person selects a morsel of food and swishes it in the stock with chopsticks until cooked. The food is dipped into one of the sauces, with a little of the spring onion added to the sesame sauce, and the onion or chili radish added to the *Ponzu*.

Skim the stock of any foam that arises during cooking. When all the ingredients have been finished, serve the remaining stock (which will have become a rich soup) in bowls with a little spring onion on top if desired.

YOSENABE

Seafood, Chicken, Vegetable and Noodle Hotpot

Yosenabe literally means a mixture of anything, so the ingredients included in this hotpot can be adjusted to suit your taste and availability. ◑◐

- $1/3$ **pound seabream fillet**
- $1/3$ **pound salmon fillet**
- $1/3$ **pound Spanish mackerel fillet**
- $1/3$ **pound chicken**
- $1/3$ **pound oysters**
- **7-inch piece** *daikon*
- $1/3$ **pound clams**
- $1/3$ **pound shrimp, peeled, tails left on and intestinal vein removed**
- **1 pound long white Chinese (Napa) cabbage**
- **4 fresh** *shiitake* **mushrooms, stems discarded and caps cross cut**
- $1/4$ **pound edible chrysanthemum leaves, hard stems removed**
- $1/4$ **pound golden or** *enoki* **(***enokitake***) mushrooms, hard ends of stems removed**
- **1 large carrot, peeled and sliced**
- **1 cup spring onions cut in** $1^1/2$**-inch lengths**
- $1/2$ **pound bean curd, cut in large dice**
- $3^1/2$ **ounces cellophane noodles, soaked until transparent**
- **Sprigs of** *kinome* **or watercress to garnish**

Stock:

- **7 cups Basic** *Dashi* **Stock (page 33)**
- $1/2$ **cup light soy sauce**
- **2 tablespoons** *mirin*

Cut the fish fillets and chicken into $1^1/4$-inch squares. Blanch each separately in boiling water until they change color, drain and set aside.

Remove the oysters from their shells and place oysters in a colander. Grate half of the *daikon* and mix gently by hand with the oysters to remove any dirt. Clean by shaking the colander in salted water. Drain and set the oysters aside. Put the clams, still in their shells, and peeled shrimp to one side.

Boil the cabbage for 2 minutes, drain and spread on a bamboo rolling mat. Roll up and squeeze tightly to remove excess moisture. Unroll and cut the cabbage roll into slices $3/4$ inch thick. Cut the chrysanthemum leaves into 2-inch to 3-inch lengths. Slice the remaining *daikon*.

Arrange all ingredients attractively on a large platter.

Prepare the **stock** by putting all ingredients into a large pan and bringing to a boil. Pour the stock into a heatproof casserole and set on a fire in the center of the table, with the platter of raw ingredients nearby. To cook, put the chicken and clams into the stock, followed by the fish, shrimp, oysters, noodles, and vegetables. Wait until the ingredients are cooked before adding the next batch of ingredients.

WANKO SOBA

Cold Buckwheat Noodles with Assorted Toppings

Noodles made from buckwheat flour (*soba*) are regarded as best eaten in a cold climate. However, the Japanese also eat cold *soba* during the summer months. ☉ ☉

> $^3/_4$ **pound dried buckwheat (*soba*) noodles**
> **2 cups *Soba Dashi* Stock (2) (page 34)**

Toppings:
> Simmered *shiitake* mushrooms (see below)
> *Tempura* fritters (see below)
> 4 teaspoons Japanese horseradish paste
> 4 heaped tablespoons finely shredded dried laver (*nori*)
> 2 eggs, lightly beaten, fried as an omelet, shredded
> 8 *shiso* leaves, shredded
> 2 spring onions, white part only, finely shredded lengthwise
> $1^1/_4$ ounces salmon or tuna, flaked
> 2 tablespoons Japanese pickles (optional)

Simmered Shiitake Mushrooms:
> 4 dried *shiitake* mushrooms
> 2 cups water
> $1^1/_2$ teaspoons sugar
> $1^1/_2$ teaspoons dark soy sauce

Tempura Fritters:
> 2 ounces burdock, peeled and cut in matchsticks $1^1/_4$ inches long
> $^1/_3$ cup sliced onion

> 1 tablespoon finely chopped *mitsuba* or parsley leaves
> $^1/_4$ cup *Tempura* Batter (page 37)
> Oil for deep frying

Prepare the **shiitake mushrooms** first by soaking the mushrooms in the water until soft. Drain and put the soaking water into a saucepan and bring to a boil. Add the mushrooms and sugar, return to a boil, skim the surface and reduce the heat. Cover and simmer gently for 40 minutes. Add the soy sauce and simmer for another 40 minutes. Allow to cool, then shred the mushrooms finely.

Boil the noodles in plenty of lightly salted water for 4–5 minutes, drain and chill in cold water. Drain again and refrigerate.

Prepare the **tempura fritters** by combining all ingredients and deep frying, a spoonful at a time, in hot oil until golden brown. Drain and keep aside.

At serving time, arrange small handfuls (enough for two mouthfuls) of the noodles in lacquer bowls. Put the remaining noodles in a basket or dish and keep on the table. Pour a little of the stock over the small bowl of noodles and add the preferred **topping**. When this is finished, add more noodles and stock to the bowl, add a different topping and continue until the noodles are used up.

ONIGIRI & ASARI NO MISO SHIRU

Rice Balls & Littleneck Clam Soup

RICE BALLS

The choice of filling inside these hearty triangular balls of steamed rice is up to the cook. The amounts in this recipe should make 12–13 rice balls. ⓓ ⓓ

5⅓ cups short-grain rice
Salt to taste
3–4 sheets of toasted laver (*nori*), cut in strips
    about 5 inches x 2 inches

Filling:

Sour plums (*umeboshi*), ½ teaspoon per rice
    ball
Cured salmon, 1 teaspoon per rice ball
Dried bonito flakes mixed with a little light soy
    sauce, 1 heaped teaspoon per rice ball
Strips of salted dried kelp (*shio-kobu*),
    1 heaped teaspoon per rice ball

Wash the rice gently under running water until the water runs clear. Leave to drain for 1 hour, then put into a saucepan with the water and bring to a boil over high heat. Reduce the heat and simmer gently for 15–20 minutes until the rice is cooked and the water absorbed. Remove from the heat, cover the rice with a towel to absorb any moisture and put back the lid. Leave to stand for 20 minutes.

To prepare the rice balls, sprinkle a little salt onto the palm of one hand and take a handful (about ½ cup of rice. Flatten it to make a depression in the center and put in a little of your chosen filling. Mold the rice to enclose the filling and shape into a triangle. Wrap with a piece of *nori* and moisten the end to seal. Set aside while preparing the remaining rice balls. Serve at room temperature.

LITTLENECK CLAM SOUP ⓓ

¾ pound littleneck or other variety of clams
1½ cups water
1½ cups Basic *Dashi* Stock (page 33)
3 tablespoons *inaka* miso
Sprigs of *mitsuba* leaves, parsley or watercress
    to garnish
Sansho powder to taste

Soak the clams in a large bowl of fresh water in a dark place for 2–3 hours to remove the sand. Lift out the clams from the bowl, taking care not to disturb the sediment, and rinse well in a bowl of fresh water. Put the clams in a saucepan with 1½ cups water and bring to a boil. Simmer until the clams open, then remove them immediately and divide among 4 lacquer soup bowls.

Add the *dashi* and *miso* to the cooking liquid left in the saucepan and stir to dissolve the *miso*. Pour over the clams and serve garnished with leaves and a sprinkle of *sansho*.

Opposite:
*Rice Balls (top)
with Litleneck
Clam Soup
(below).*

ANSAI GOHAN & TOFU TO NAMEKO NO MISO SHIRU

Rice with Mountain Vegetables & Miso Soup with Mushrooms

RICE WITH MOUNTAIN VEGETABLES

Mountain vegetables, a mixture of bracken, fiddle-head fern tips and *nameko* mushrooms, are packed in water and sold in plastic bags or glass jars. They have a wonderful "woodsy" flavor and interesting texture that transforms plain rice into a treat. ⏱

Opposite:
*Rice with
Mountain
Vegetables (right)
and Miso Soup
with Mushrooms
(above center)*.

$1^{1}/_{3}$ **cups short-grain rice**
$1^{1}/_{2}$ **cups water**
$^{1}/_{2}$ **ounce thin fried bean curd (*aburage*)**
7 ounces mountain vegetables, drained

Seasoning for Mountain Vegetables:
2 teaspoons *sake*
2 teaspoons light soy sauce

Seasoning for Rice:
1 teaspoon salt
2 teaspoons *sake*
1 teaspoon light soy sauce
1 teaspoon *mirin*

Wash the rice gently under running water until the water runs clear. Put the rice and the $1^{1}/_{2}$ cups water in a saucepan and soak for 20 minutes.

Pour boiling water on both sides of the fried bean curd to remove excess oil. Cut in half lengthwise, and cut each piece into $^{1}/_{2}$-inch-wide strips.

Mix the **seasoning for mountain vegetables** with the drained vegetables and let stand for 5 minutes. Mix the vegetables and fried bean curd strips into the rice together with its soaking water. Add the **seasoning for rice**, stir gently, cover the pan and bring to a boil over high heat. Reduce the heat and simmer gently for 15–20 minutes until the rice is cooked and the water absorbed. Remove from the heat, cover the rice with a towel to absorb any moisture and put back the lid. Leave to stand for 20 minutes and serve hot.

MISO SOUP WITH MUSHROOMS

Nameko mushrooms, attractive reddish-brown little fungi with a slippery texture, are excellent fresh, although the bottled or canned variety could be used in this soup if fresh *nameko* are not available. ⏱

3 cups Basic *Dashi* Stock (page 33)
$^{1}/_{4}$ **cup *inaka miso***
1 ounce *nameko* mushrooms, rinsed
5 ounces silken bean curd, finely diced
4 teaspoons very finely sliced spring onions

Put the *dashi* into a saucepan and bring to a boil. Add the *miso*, stirring to dissolve. Put in the mushrooms and bean curd and heat, but do not allow to boil. Pour the soup into 4 lacquer soup bowls and sprinkle each portion with 1 teaspoon of spring onions.

OCHAZUKE & TEMPURA SOBA

Rice with Green Tea & Buckwheat Noodles with Tempura

RICE WITH GREEN TEA ⏱

4 bowls (about 2¹⁄₂ cups) steamed rice
4 heaped tablespoons salted salmon flakes
4 tablespoons finely shredded toasted laver
  (*nori*)
1–2 *shiso* leaves, shredded, or 4 tablespoons
  finely sliced spring onion
2 teaspoons Japanese horseradish paste
2–3 cups hot Japanese green tea or Basic *Dashi*
  Stock (page 33)

Divide the rice among 4 rice bowls and top each with 1 tablespoon salmon, 1 tablespoon *nori* and one-quarter of the *shiso* leaves or spring onions. Top each portion with ¹⁄₂ teaspoon of horseradish paste and pour in enough hot tea or *dashi* to come to the top of the rice in each bowl.

BUCKWHEAT NOODLES WITH
TEMPURA ⏱⏱

12 cups water
1 teaspoon salt
9 ounces buckwheat (soba) noodles
4 cups *Soba Dashi* Stock (1) (page 34)
4 teaspoons finely sliced spring onion
Seven-spice powder (*shichimi*) to taste

Tempura:
8 medium-sized shrimp
1 heaped tablespoon flour

4 fresh *shiitake* mushrooms, stems discarded
  and caps cross cut
4 *shiso* leaves
²⁄₃ cup *Tempura* Batter (page 37)
Oil for deep frying

Bring the water and salt to a boil and add the noodles. Boil uncovered for 4–5 minutes, until the noodles are cooked. Drain, chill in iced water and drain again.

Put the stock into a saucepan and bring to a boil. Keep warm while preparing the *tempura*.

To prepare the **tempura**, peel the shrimp, discarding the head but leaving on the tail. Split open down the back, remove intestinal tract and press the shrimp open gently with the hand to make a butterfly shape. Dip the shrimp into flour, shake, dip into the batter and deep fry until golden brown and cooked. Drain. Dip the *shiitake* mushrooms and *shiso* leaves in batter and deep fry. Drain.

Put the cooked noodles back into the stock and reheat. Divide the noodles among 4 bowls. Taste the stock and season with salt if needed, then pour over the noodles. Top each portion of noodles with 2 shrimp, 1 mushroom and 1 *shiso* leaf and garnish each with 1 teaspoon of spring onion and a little seven-spice powder.

TOMATO BURANDI-FUMI & MATCHA AISUKURIIMU

Tomato Simmered with Cognac & Green-tea Ice Cream

TOMATO SIMMERED WITH COGNAC

A curious sounding dessert, this modern Japanese dish is the creation of Takayuki Kosaki, of the Hyatt Regency, Osaka. It is simple to make, visually appealing and surprisingly good to eat. 🕐

- 4 medium-large tomatoes, weighing about $\frac{1}{4}$ pound each
- 3 cups water
- 1 cup sugar, or slightly more to taste
- 1 teaspoon salt
- 2 tablespoons cognac or brandy, or more to taste

Opposite: Tomato Simmered with Cognac (right) and Green-tea Ice Cream (left).

Blanch the tomatoes in a large pan of boiling water for about 15 seconds, remove and place in the cold water. As soon as the tomatoes are cool enough to handle, peel.

Put the 3 cups water, sugar and salt into a large saucepan and bring to a boil. Add the tomatoes and simmer gently until they are tender. Remove from the heat, add the cognac and leave to cool. Refrigerate until serving in a glass bowl with a little syrup around each tomato.

GREEN-TEA ICE CREAM

A popular summertime dessert in Japanese restaurants, this might be termed a "modern classic." Finely powdered green tea gives a uniquely Japanese flavor to this delightfully rich ice cream. 🕐🕐

- $1\frac{1}{2}$ ounces green tea powder (about 6 tablespoons)
- $\frac{1}{2}$ cup cognac or brandy
- 5 cups fresh milk
- 1 cup fresh cream
- $1\frac{1}{3}$ cups instant nonfat dry milk powder
- $1\frac{3}{4}$ cups sugar

Put the green tea powder into a bowl, add the cognac and mix well. Put the milk, cream, sugar and dry milk powder into another bowl and mix well. Transfer to a saucepan and bring to a boil over moderate heat. Remove from the heat and allow to cool to a lukewarm temperature, then add the green tea paste, mixing well.

Chill immediately in the freezer portion of the refrigerator until ice crystals start to form around the edges of the container. Put the mixture into a blender or food processor and blend for a few seconds to break up the crystals. Return to the freezer and leave until set. Alternatively, freeze in an ice-cream maker according to the manufacturer's instructions.

DORA-YAKI & KINGYOKU-KAN

Red-bean Pancakes & Jellied Plums

RED-BEAN PANCAKES

Very popular in Japan and sold hot at stalls everywhere, these pancakes can be found with a variety of fillings, including Western-style custard. Red bean is, however, the traditional favorite. ◑ ◔

> 2 cups white flour
> 4 teaspoons sugar
> 1 cup water
> 1 egg white, beaten until fluffy white
> Oil to grease pan
> 6 ounces red-bean jam, sieved

Opposite:
Red-bean
Pancakes (top left)
and Jellied Plums
(below right).

Sift the flour into a bowl and add the sugar. Stir in the water to make a batter, then fold in the egg white. Heat a frying pan (preferably nonstick) and grease lightly with oil. Drop about $1\frac{1}{2}$ tablespoons of the batter into the pan, letting it spread by itself. When tiny bubbles begin to form on the pancake surface, turn over. Fry for 30 seconds, then remove. Make another pancake in the same fashion. Spread red bean jam onto one pancake and cover with the second pancake. Repeat until all the batter is used up.

JELLIED PLUMS

A simple but decorative dessert, with large grapes or plums set in jellied plum wine (*umeshu*). If the plum wine is not available in a Japanese store, substitute any fruit wine, such as peach or raspberry. ◑ ◔

> 8 large black or white grapes, or small plums
> $1\frac{1}{2}$ cups wine (*umeshu*) or substitute (see above)
> $2\frac{1}{2}$ envelopes unflavored gelatin
> $\frac{1}{4}$ cup warm water
> $2\frac{1}{2}$ tablespoons sugar
> 1 teaspoon cognac or brandy

Blanch the grapes or plums in hot water for about 10 seconds, drain and put in cold water to chill for a few seconds. Peel and set aside.

Sprinkle the gelatin over the warm water and leave until it softens. Heat the wine in a nonreactive saucepan and add sugar and gelatin. Stir until dissolved, then remove from the heat. Add the cognac and pour into 8 tiny containers (such as ramekins or small porcelain soup bowls). Put 1 grape or plum into each bowl of still-liquid jelly, then chill until the jelly is firm. Unmold and serve chilled.

SAKURA MOCHI & CHAKIN-SHIBORI
Cherry Blossom Dumplings & Lily Bulb Dumplings

CHERRY BLOSSOM DUMPLINGS

Wrapped in cherry leaves, these dumplings filled with red-bean jam are inevitably associated with spring time or *sakura*. If you can't find edible cherry leaves packed in brine, the dumplings can be served without them. ① ①

- 1 cup white flour
- 2 teaspoons sugar
- $^1/_2$ cup water
- $^1/_2$ egg white, beaten until fluffy and white
- Pinch of salt
- Oil to grease pan lightly
- $3^1/_2$ ounces red-bean jam
- 8 cherry blossom leaves (soaked in water for 2 hours if using brine-soaked leaves)

Sift flour into a bowl and add the sugar. Add water a little at a time. Fold in the egg white and salt. Lightly grease a nonstick frying pan and put over low heat. Spread in some of the batter into an oval shape. Cook until the top of the dumpling becomes dry and turn over. Cook on the second side but do not allow the dumpling to take color. Remove the dumpling, spread with red bean jam. Fold over and wrap with a cherry blossom leaf.

Opposite:
Cherry Blossom Dumplings (right) and Lily Bulb Dumplings (left).

LILY BULB DUMPLINGS

The sweet, nutty flavor and floury texture of lily bulbs, which are readily available in Japan during the winter months, go well with a red-bean filling in these quickly made dumplings. An alternative to the lily bulb is sweet potato. ①

- $^3/_4$ pound lily bulb or sweet potato
- $^1/_4$ cup sugar
- $2^1/_2$ ounces red-bean jam, strained
- 2 tablespoons finely grated *yuzu* orange or lemon peel

Separate the lily bulb, which looks somewhat like a head of garlic, into petals. Put the petals onto a plate and steam for about 3 minutes or until soft. Drain. Alternatively, steam the unpeeled sweet potatoes whole, then drain and peel.

Mash the steamed vegetable, then mix with sugar and knead well. Shape about 2 tablespoons of the purée into a dumpling and fill with a teaspoon of red-bean jam. Shape into a dumpling by putting the ball into a cloth and squeezing gently at the top. Remove from the cloth and sprinkle with grated peel. Repeat until all the purée is used up, then serve.

Mail-order Sources of Ingredients

The ingredients used in this book can all be found in markets featuring the foods of Japan. Many of them can also be found in markets featuring Asian foods, as well as any well-stocked supermarket.

Health food stores often stock *tamari*, soy sauce, *tofu*, seaweed and numerous fresh vegetables that are used frequently in Japanese recipes, including *daikon*. Ingredients not found locally may be available from the mail-order markets listed below.

Adriana's Caravan
409 Vanderbilt Street
Brooklyn, NY 11218
Tel: 800-316-0820 or 718-436-8565

Anzen Importers
736 NE Union Ave.
Portland, OR 97232
Tel: 503-233-5111

Central Market
40th & Lamar St.
Austin, Texas
Tel: 512-206-1000

Frieda's-By-Mail
Frieda's Inc.
4465 Corporate Center Drive
Los Alamitos, CA 90720-2561
Tel: 800-241-1771

Gourmail, Inc.
816 Newton Road
Berwyn, PA 19312
Tel: 215-296-4620

House of Spices
76-17 Broadway
Jackson Heights
Queens, NY 11373
Tel: 718-507-4900

Kam Man Food Products
200 Canal Street
New York, NY 10013
Tel: 212-755-3566

Nancy's Specialty Market
P.O. Box 1302
Stamford, CT 06904
Tel: 800-462-6291

Oriental Food Market and Cooking School
2801 Howard St.
Chicago, IL 60645
Tel: 312-274-2826

Oriental Market
502 Pampas Drive
Austin, TX 78752
Tel: 512-453-9058

Pacific Mercantile Company, Inc.
1925 Lawrence St.
Denver, CO 80202
Tel: 303-295-0293

Rafal Spice Company
2521 Russell
Detroit, MI 48207
Tel: 313-259-6373

Spice House
1048 N. Old World 3rd St.
Milwaukee, WI
Tel: 414-272-0977

Uwajimaya
PO Box 3003
Seattle, WA 98114
Tel: 206-624-6248

Vietnam Imports
922 W. Broad Street
Falls Church, VA 22046
Tel: 703-534-9441

Index

131